UNIONS

FOR BEGINNERS®

UNIONS

FOR BEGINNERS®

DAVID COGSWELL • ILLUSTRATIONS BY C.M. BUTZER

FOR BEGINNERS®

an imprint of Steerforth Press

Hanover, New Hampshire

For Beginners LLC
155 Main Street, Suite 211
Danbury, CT 06810 USA
www.forbeginnersbooks.com

A For Beginners® Documentary Comic Book

Cataloging-in-Publication information is available from the Library of Congress.

ISBN # 978-1-934389-77-5 Trade

Manufactured in the United States of America

For Beginners® and Beginners Documentary Comic Books® are published by For Beginners LLC.

First Edition

10 9 8 7 6 5 4 3 2 1

Table of Contents

Preface

This book is being written at a time of tremendous social upheaval in America and around the world. America seems to have reached the proverbial tipping point when one movement reaches its limit and the pendulum begins to swing back in the opposite direction. Thirty years after the Reagan Revolution started the trend toward the rich getting richer and corporations gaining ever more power over American life, the people have started to push back. Every day things are happening that seem to have the potential to affect the course of history. The Occupy Wall Street movement against the economic injustice of the global corporate system that began in Lower Manhattan is spreading around the world.

These events will continue to play out after this book goes to press and no one can predict their future course. It does seem, however, that certain trends are set and are not likely to be reversed. After a long period of ascendance of corporate power in America, people are fighting back. When confronted by the same problems approached by working people in the Gilded Age 100 years previously, people are returning to some of the same solutions they turned to in those days. Primary among them is the formation of unions, the banding together of people in pursuit of a common goal of justice and fairness from those who own and control a disproportionate amount of the resources of the country and the world.

When we read histories of unions we read about people who worked in factories or agricultural fields with tough working conditions and people who lived close to the edge of survival. We believe we have come a long way from that now. We have fewer people in factories, more in office jobs. But the crash of 2008 put millions out of work and/or out of their homes and into poverty, while Wall Street banking firms, whose irresponsible practices brought on the crash, received taxpayer bailouts and then their profits soared. We see that many of the same problems that came down on working people 100 years ago are back, though wearing different clothing. Under the surface of changing times and styles the issues are much the same for office workers as for factory workers: low pay, lack of benefits, too much work for too little share of the profits. In the first decade of the 21st Century, as the wealth of the country has fallen under the control of a smaller and smaller elite group, regular people have been grasping at straws trying to figure out how to fight back, how to recover a foothold in the economic system. As much of the middle class has fallen through the cracks into unemployment, poverty and homelessness, many have nothing better to do anymore than to take to the streets and finally confront the economic and political problems in an existential way, with their own bodies. Many Americans now find that their backs are to the wall, and they have few options.

The natural inclination of human beings in trouble is to band together with others in the same predicament to fight for their rights, freedom from oppression, fairness and justice. And that brings us to the story of labor unions. Unions are based on people joining forces to fight against oppression and for their fair share.

It's a long and varied story, a broad tapestry of human history with its own heroes and villains. Unions have not always been good for their members or their communities. Sometimes they have gone off the tracks in terms of ethical and responsible behavior. Union leaders have sometimes failed their memberships, or have been corrupted by their power and taken too much from the membership in return for too little. All the frailties of human nature apply to unions as they do in other spheres of life. Mainly unions have helped to improve the lives of millions of people, including those who are not members of unions but still benefitted from the rising standards of working conditions. And though unions have faded from the scene in American life in the last half century, there are signs that the time of union ascendance is back again.

Chris Hedges, a Pulitzer Prize winning reporter who was a war correspondent for the *New York Times* for 15 years, attended the Occupy Wall Street protests in Lower Manhattan a week or so after they began September 17, 2011. In an interview from the scene he explained why he was there, why the gathering of people to protest is so important and why America's working people, including its middle class, must again band together in unions to protect themselves against an assault by the power elite of the country.

"I just got back from Immokalee, Florida," said Hedges, "where the Coalition of Immokalee Workers is about to begin a campaign against supermarkets like Trader Joe's, Stop n Shop, and Giant, which is extremely important because if it succeeds it will probably double the wages, which run between eight and ten thousand dollars for agricultural workers in the fields who work in horrific conditions at best and at worst conditions that resemble slavery. But I've been following what's been happening here and this is really where the hope of America lies. And all of the efforts of intimidation that we've seen by the police in New York, the disproportionate amount of force and the disproportionate numbers that have been deployed to contain the protests here, for me illustrate that the real people who are scared are the power elite. Of course they're trying to make you scared and us scared, but I can tell you having been a reporter for the *New York Times* that inside they are very very frightened. They do not want movements like this to grow. And they understand on some level, whether it's subconscious or overt, that the criminal class in this country has seized power, that those people in this plaza, the people carrying out these protests, in the true political spectrum are conservatives in this sense. They call for the rule of law. They call for the restoration of the rule of law. And what's happened is that the real radicals have seized power and they are decimating all impediments to the creation of a neo-feudalistic corporate city, one in which there is a rapacious oligarchic class, a thin managerial elite, and two thirds of this country live in conditions that increasingly push families to the subsistence level.

"And one of the reasons I went to Immokalee and the reasons Immokalee is important is because in this race to the bottom Immokalee is the bottom. It's where they want the working and even the middle class to end up, and that is a place where they have no rights, where because of massive unemployment and work that is part time poorly paid work, they can reduce the working class to a status equivalent to serfdom, where there are no pensions, no health benefits. Collective Bargaining in Florida is illegal, a legacy of Jim Crow. And Immokalee isn't just a horrific pocket of essentially Third World abuse, but is the vision of what the corporate state wants to impose upon the rest of us. What they want is for us to remain passive and to remain frightened. As long as we remain passive and frightened and entranced by their electronic hallucinations we are not a threat. The moment people come out and do this the corporate state is terrified, and if you doubt me, look around you at the huge numbers of cops and not only that, the brutality they have visited on peaceful protesters."

Introduction

The Twilight of the Unions

"Those who do not remember the past are doomed to repeat it."
— George Santayana

According to the U.S. Bureau of Labor Statistics, in 2010 the percentage of wage and salary workers who were members of unions was 11.9 percent, down from 12.3 percent the previous year. Union membership reached its peak in the late 1950s when about a third of American workers were members of unions. In 1955, the rate of union membership in the public sector was 36.2 percent (7.6 million). In the private sector it was only 6.9 percent (7.1 million).

George Santayana

E.J. Dionne, a writer for the Washington Post, writes, "Even worse than the falling membership numbers is the extent to which the ethos animating organized labor is increasingly foreign to American culture. The union movement has always been attached to a set of values — solidarity being the most important, the sense that each should look out for the interests of all. This promoted other commitments: to mutual assistance, to a rough-and-ready sense of equality, to a disdain for elitism, to a belief that democracy and individual rights did not stop at the plant gate or the office reception room."

In 2011, after a Republican sweep in the midyear elections during Obama's presidency, Republican governors joined together in an effort to squash unions in the public sector across the country. It started in Wisconsin and swept across the Republican-controlled states. Governor Scott Walker of Wisconsin and his Republican-controlled state legislature passed legislation that took away the right of public employees to be represented by collective bargaining. Soon after passing the law, Walker started replacing state workers with prison inmates.

This coordinated assault on unions and on the right of workers to be represented collectively came at a time of great economic pressure following the crash of 2008 and what came to be known as the Great Recession, which settled in and would not go away. Major banks and financial institutions, whose irresponsible behavior brought on the financial collapse, were bailed out with taxpayer money. Wall Street and the financial sector bounced back quickly to its former trend of soaring profits and huge salaries and bonuses. Meanwhile, for the vast majority of Americans things did not improve much from the depths of the recession. Unemployment stayed historically high.

Naomi Klein, author of *The Shock Doctrine* showed how the right wing has learned to exploit crises by using them as opportunities to ram through parts of the agenda they are always pushing for anyway. "It should not be in any way surprising that we are seeing right-wing ideologues across the country using economic crisis as a pretext to really wage a kind of a final battle in a 50-year war against trade unions, where we've seen membership in trade unions drop precipitously," she said in an interview. "And public sector unions are the last labor stronghold, and they're going after it. And these governors did not run elections promising to do these radical actions, but they are using the pretext of crisis to do things that they couldn't get elected promising to do."

After an initial economic stimulus pushed through by President Obama to invest in creating jobs through infrastructural development, to spark consumer demand and get the money circulating again, the political and media elite turned away from the unemployed and started focusing on paying down the deficit. The deficit had grown to its highest levels in history during the administration of George W. Bush, when he initiated tax cuts for the wealthiest Americans and corporations and launched two expensive wars, which rang up a bill of $3 trillion (that's three million millions or three thousand billions). The final blow was the global financial collapse that resulted from wildly corrupt practices in the financial sector, and the nearly trillion-dollar taxpayer bailouts, which were initiated under Bush. The financial institutions were given additional trillions from the Federal Reserve, which has the power to create money.

The first-ever accounting of the Federal Reserve by the General Accounting Office revealed in 2011 that the Federal Reserve had issued $16 trillion in secret bank bailouts. According to Dennis Kucinich, a U.S. representative from Ohio, "With 14 million people out of work, and the government saying well, we can't create any programs because we can't afford it, we're missing something that is fundamental to our economy, and that is that while the Fed has been busy creating over $2 trillion for banks since the fall of 2008 through programs like Quantitative Easing [Rounds] 1 and 2, and you've got banks that got $700 billion in bailouts and they, too, can create money out of nothing through fractional reserve banking—meanwhile, we're being told that the government can't do that. Well, actually, it's a sovereign power that resides in the government: the ability to coin or create money."

The Republicans under Bush had gleefully participated in running up the deficit to their highest levels ever. Then suddenly after Obama became president, they became supposedly very concerned about the deficit and federal spending. They wanted to start a new season of austerity, not for themselves of course, not for the big spenders on Wall Street that the taxpayers had to bail out, but for the taxpayers themselves, the working people of America, those whose tax dollars had bailed out the giant financial institutions who were deemed "too big to fail." After the taxpayers of America had bailed out the largest banking firms, the Republicans who held a majority in Congress decided they were going to pay the bill for the bailout by ending Social Security and Medicare, which would leave many older Americans with no means of support, literally in many cases to leave them to die.

After trillions of dollars of public money had been given to massive financial institutions deemed "too big to fail," and in many cases guilty of fraud and stealing, the legislators proceeded to try to balance the budget, to pay for the crash and the bank bailouts by taking money out of Social Security, Medicare, Medicaid and virtually any other program that provides services or support for the people.

Americans who have paid into the Social Security system all their lives were being told by politicians that the money they had paid into the system would not necessarily be there when they needed it. Meanwhile the same legislators refused to raise any taxes on the highest earners in the company, who had received huge tax cuts at the beginning of Bush's term before he went on to squander $3 trillion on wars in Afghanistan and Iraq. Giant corporations were allowed to take advantage of tax loopholes that allowed them to make tens of billions of dollars without paying any tax at all.

A group of citizen activists calling themselves Occupy Washington DC produced an alternative budget proposal in November 2011. It was a way to balance the budget without cutting essential services like Social Security and Medicare. The report outlined the tax rates in America since 1944.

"The United States does not have a lack of financial resources," said the report, "it has an intentionally unfair distribution of resources. The federal income tax has become less progressive and the rate paid by the wealthiest has been cut dramatically in recent decades. From 1944 through 1951, the highest marginal tax rate for individuals was 91 percent, increasing to 92 percent for 1952 and 1953, and reverting to 91 percent for tax years 1954 through 1963. In 1964, the top marginal tax rate for individuals was 77 percent. From 1965 through 1981 the top rate was 70 percent. The top marginal tax rate was lowered to 50 percent for tax years 1982 through 1986 and today it is just 35 percent. The tax on investment income, capital gains, has also been dramatically reduced. The maximum statutory rate on long-term capital gains was 28 percent in 1991, 20 percent in 1997 and has been merely 15 percent since 2003."

The report went on to say, "The wealth divide has become extreme over the past three decades and tax policies have exacerbated this trend; much of the tax code exemplifies policies for the 1 percent at the expense of the 99 percent. The wealth divide is one of the foundational reasons why the economy no longer works and is in steady decline for most people in the United States. The tax code inadequately funds government, but that is the result of unfair tax cuts, not because America is broke (it isn't). As Andrew Fieldhouse of the Economic Policy Institute testified, 'Income per capita has jumped 66 percent over the past 30 years, and is projected to grow another 60 percent over the next 30 years.' The country needs to put in place policies that reduce the wealth divide and share wealth fairly so that when the economy grows it benefits all citizens, not just the 1 percent."
The American middle class found itself the victim of a massive swindle. By a few broad strokes of legislative accounting, the

elected officials of Washington moved the assets of the country from the middle class to the wealthiest sectors of corporate America. Then when the budget was broken, they wanted to balance it by taking more from the people who bailed out the bankers, the taxpayers, rank-and-file Americans.

While the elected officials in Washington eagerly serve the interests of their corporate donors and ignore the wishes of the majority of their constituents, working conditions, salaries and benefits and a whole range of quality of life metrics across the country are in decline. While Wall Street profits continue to soar, the salaries and wages of the vast majority had stayed flat for decades. The working people of America have been abandoned. They have no representatives in Washington. What happened? Is there no longer any champion of the people?

Unions and Quality of Life

As increasing numbers of suddenly struggling, impoverished, unemployed and homeless Americans ask themselves what happened, it is inevitable that the history of the unions would once again become a matter of great interest. In fact, the history of unions reads very much like a prescription for what ails the country today.

The history of labor unions and their contribution to the quality of life of Americans and to the growth of a strong middle class is practically forgotten. Few people today seem to even know what unions are, or were, and what their significance has been in American history.

As the unions have declined in influence, the quality of life of the majority of Americans has also declined. A study released in 2010 funded by the private philanthropy Foundation for Child Development and conducted by Duke University found that the economic well being of families in America had declined sharply, returning to levels not seen since 1975. Kenneth Land, the project coordinator and professor of sociology and demography at Duke University told CNN, "Virtually all of that progress is wiped out through job losses, through declines in real income, and other aspects of family economic well-being,"

The study was based on predictions about 28 indicators that include economic well-being, social relationships, community engagement, educational attainment and health. In 2010 500,000 children were homeless, 750,000 were living in food-insecure homes. A lack of access to healthier foods by poor people means that health is also in decline in these populations.

As the labor movement has reached a twilight in America, working conditions for the majority are declining rapidly. The majority of Americans, the working people, are seeing their salaries declining relative to the cost of living. Their benefits are disappearing, job security is diminishing. Millions of Americans have no access to affordable healthcare. And most find themselves alone in their struggle to get a fair deal from powerful corporations that employ them. Many of these Americans are beginning to wonder about the history of the unions. That history that is all but forgotten or never known by most Americans is suddenly becoming urgently relevant. As working conditions decline to a level reminiscent of a century ago, more people are getting curious about what the unions were, and what they brought to American life.

According to Steve Fraser, writing at TomDispatch.com, "One in every three Americans is now considered either poor or 'near poor,' according to recent census data; that is, 49.1 million Americans are below the poverty line and another 51 million perilously close to it. This, of course, represents a significant increase in downward mobility. According to the New York Times, 'over half of the near poor in the new tally actually fell into that group from higher income levels as their resources were sapped by medical expenses, taxes, work-related costs and other unavoidable outlays.'"

As union membership has declined in America, the once-healthy and growing middle class has lost ground. While the top five percent of the wealthy have seen their fortunes mushroom in value, the great majority has seen its actual spending power and quality of life go down. The fact that the rise and decline of unions mirrors the rise and decline of the American middle class does not necessarily mean that the middle class fell because the unions fell. But let's look a little closer at that relationship.

A list of the things unions have fought for includes pay increases, health benefits, shorter hours, retirement benefits and of course the weekend. The labor movement has also fought for and helped to win legislation that arguably improves the lives of millions of people who are not affiliated with unions, and may have no idea how the unions have benefitted them. These include maternity leave, occupational health and safety regulations, Medicare, paid annual leave and the right to collective bargaining.

In many of these areas regarding the common welfare of the majority of the population, the U.S. lags behind most other countries in the developed world. But now the American people are losing ground even in comparison to what they had previously.

American working people are losing the ground that many people fought and some even died for in the history of the labor movement.

It was unions that fought for those benefits, for the weekend, for wages that could support families and give working people a chance to own their own homes and cars and improve their lives and partake of the prosperity of the country. Not to say that unions and union leaders have always been good. It's not a black and white history. Unions have existed in many forms in response to many different kinds of situations.

Bringing Balance to Society

Unions bring value to all sectors of a society. As the champion of people power versus corporate power, Unions help to spread the benefits of production throughout a society. When employees earn more money, they become consumers, and consumer spending is the driving engine of the economy. Economies are measured by their consumption. When you cut salaries, you hold the economy back, stifle its growth.

Unions also push up salaries and benefits for the society at large, not just union members. Unions help to keep a society democratic and lawful. They help to stop corporate power from trampling on human rights. There is no separation between the union movement and the larger human rights movement. Martin Luther King, Jr. recognized this affinity.

In 1961, he wrote "If the Negro Wins, Labor Wins," in which he says: "Negroes in the United States read the history of labor and find it mirrors their own experience. We are confronted by powerful forces telling us to rely on the good will and understanding of those who profit by exploiting us.... They are shocked that action organizations, sit-ins, civil disobedience and protests are becoming our everyday tools, just as strikes, demonstrations and union organization became yours to insure that bargaining power genuinely existed on both sides of the table... Our needs are identical to labor's needs: decent wages, fair working conditions, livable housing, old age security, health and welfare measures... That is why the labor-hater and labor-baiter is virtually always a twin-headed creature spewing anti-Negro epithets from one mouth and anti-labor propaganda from the other mouth."

Strength in numbers

Unions are based on one of the most elemental principles in human life: strength in numbers. When primitive hunters wanted to bring down a huge beast, they found they could do it if enough of them worked together. It's fundamental that you are stronger when you are joined by other people who share your interests. Unions were the associations created by working people to represent their interests as a group in their relationships with wealthy industrialists.

Unions historically have been founded on a set of principles. At the heart of them is solidarity, the idea of people looking out for each other's interests. Unions also embody fundamental democratic values, such as equal rights and a rejection of elitism.

Unions created many benefits for the American people. The labor movement was largely responsible for creating the middle class, and for creating a consumer class, a wide segment of the population that could afford to buy the products of American manufacturers and help to keep their businesses thriving.

In the early 21st Century, a rising number of people have lost their retirement funds or their homes, seen their net worth crumble and their buying power diminished, and in general have seen the American dream of prosperity pulled away from them by mysterious, veiled forces said to be "too big to fail" and apparently too big to oppose. For those who are seeking a solution to their loss of economic and political power, a study of the unions and the labor movement is a good place to begin.

Chapter One

The Labor Movement—What Is It?

In the Beginning ... there were no labor unions.

The labor movement is the historical progression of working people joining forces to bargain with their employers for better working or living conditions, such as better hours and better pay. The labor movement may be seen as a part of the larger historical march of human beings toward human rights, self determination and justice. It is part of the long struggle of individuals banding together to defend themselves against tyranny and illegitimate authority.

The labor movement is not one single, coherent movement. It is a history of many diverse people struggling for their own interests, banding together to achieve their objectives in various ways. The history has had many twists and turns. Over and over again, unions have made gains, then alternately suffered losses. Unions have had their problems struggling with management, and they have had their own problems from within.

But overall, unions in America have contributed greatly to the general welfare of the people and have helped create advances in the quality of life for large numbers of people. Unions have helped create balance between the rich and poor, and an economy that functions well for rich and poor because they have helped working people have money to spend to buy products and keep their producers in business. The benefits unions have created for their workers have also helped other workers who are not members of unions by raising the standards for all. The work of unions has helped to create the middle class. And, conversely, the decline of unions has precipitated a fall of the middle class.

What defines a union is people banding together, uniting, to combine forces to bring some power to bear on employers to force them to share more of their profits with workers. As such they have become an important part of the functioning of democracy. Unions have been the vehicle for working Americans to fight for themselves against the forces of big money who own the businesses and largely control the political system.

Collective Bargaining: How Unions Achieve Their Goals

The essential principle behind unions is collective bargaining. People who share the same interests will naturally join together to fight for their shared interests. And their power as a group will be greater than their power as individuals. Collective bargaining is the tool by which working people without the power of capital or ownership fight for justice against those who hold the capital and power in society. Collective bargaining is one of the ways democratic societies are built.

Collective bargaining may be a discussion over a negotiating table, but usually that occurs only when other kinds of action have forced the employers to the bargaining table. Usually direct action taken by unions uses as leverage the ultimate purpose of corporations: creating profit. From a strictly business point of view, businesses exist primarily to create profit. But it is arguable that business is about more than making money. As Fezziwig in Charles Dickens' *A Christmas Carol* said, "Money is not the only reason one has a business. One has a business to maintain a way of life that one knew and loved." A newspaper publisher may love publishing and providing news and information to his community. A clothing manufacturer may enjoy creating the best clothes in the market. But as businesses get larger and become corporations, they are increasingly motivated by profit only.

In fact, corporations are mandated by law to maximize shareholder value and that alone, and that means make as much profit as possible. There is no other purpose for the existence of corporations under existing corporate law. Workers with a grievance cannot appeal to the sympathy of the corporation. Corporations, though legally defined as people, are not people — they do not have hearts or souls. And though they are owned and directed by people who may have human feelings, the directors of a public corporation are legally mandated to pursue only one goal, that of increasing profit. So the only way to appeal to a corporation is through its profits. Anything that threatens to reduce profits, whether it is a strike or work stoppage, losing too many employees, low employee morale or inciting public anger, can be an effective bargaining chip when dealing with the corporation.

Companies that are not public corporations may have more interest in other humanitarian values. And when they do, there is seldom a need for unions or collective bargaining actions. But for the most part, profit is what business is about in a capitalist society, and profit is the primary fulcrum upon which workers can exert power over employers.

A Pillar of Democracy

The U.S. Constitution names the free press as an essential part of maintaining a democratic society. The free press is not an official part of government, it is free and independent by its very nature, but the Constitution calls it the Fourth Estate. The Constitution names three branches of government: the judicial, the legislative and the executive branch. And then it designates the free press as the Fourth Estate. The press is not part of the government, but essential nevertheless for the maintenance of a democratic society.

Unions are also not named in the Constitution, but have come to be recognized as an essential force in maintaining the balance between the collective power of capital in a corporation and the general population. As such unions are an essential part of maintaining what the Constitution names in its opening paragraph as one of the essential reasons for the creation of a government: promoting the general welfare.

Unions and the General Welfare

The purpose of government is defined by the document that created the U.S. government, the U.S. Constitution. The first paragraph of the Constitution says, "We the People of the United States, in Order to form a more perfect Union, establish Justice, insure domestic Tranquility, provide for the common defense, promote the general Welfare, and secure the Blessings of Liberty to ourselves and our Posterity, do ordain and establish this Constitution for the United States of America."

As the country evolved and corporations became stronger and wielded more power in society, they became more oppressive (power corrupts). To defend themselves, working people banded together. Unions became an important part of the maintenance of economic democracy, without which there can be no political democracy.

Nelson Lichtenstein, a professor and labor historian at the University of California Santa Barbara, writes, "If you look at the last 150 years of history across all nations with a working class of some sort, the maintenance of democracy and the maintenance of a union movement are joined at the hip. If democracy has a future, then so, too, must trade unionism."

Political columnist Stephen Herrington wrote that, "Labor unions are not optional. Unions exist for a natural tidal socioeconomic reason in balance to and because of capitalism, and they are an integral part of the success of capitalism."

Nelson Lichtenstein

The hardcore right wing industrialists, like the ubiquitous Koch brothers, David and Charles, push for a world in which there are no unions and they can do whatever they want with no resistance from employees. But in fact the big capitalists would also suffer from a collapse of economic balance in society. If the workers have no money to spend, the big capitalists have no one to buy their products. In the early 21st Century, multinational corporations no longer have as much stake in maintaining a middle class in America because they can find markets in the rich sectors of other countries. But as the Great Recession kicked off by the global financial meltdown enveloped the world, the economic slowdown took over virtually the whole planet.

As Republicans try to enrich their rich donors by destroying union resistance to their profit-seeking activities, and to protect the rich from having to pay taxes, they are tearing apart the foundations of civil and economic society. "If people are poor they only buy staples," explains Herrington. "If governments are poor they can't accomplish collective goals. Commerce is layered on top of these two fundamental behaviors of peoples. You may want to create something wonderful, but without a public sufficiently wealthy to buy it, your iPad will be a street corner vendor's curiosity show instead of a multi-billion dollar market."

This is the underlying problem with the Great Recession of 2008. The American middle class has fallen so far in spending power, and has used up all its credit, so that it is no longer able to drive the economy through consumer spending. For multinational corporations, the failure of the U.S. economy is not a problem unless it affects their profits adversely. And so far during Great Recession they have shown that it doesn't. As the middle class collapses, corporate profits continue to soar. Major corporations have no national loyalties. They are multinational by definition, and seek only profit, according to the corporate mandate.

However, for the American people, for whom the state of the economy and "general welfare" does matter, the destruction of the unions is disastrous. According to Herrington, "Economies are measured by what they consume. There is no other measure because there is no other reality... The highest median consuming publics, the largest economies, are those in which the populations are more highly paid. Economies are built on the median income of their citizens. It's not rational to believe otherwise. But the combined forces of increasingly irrational capitalism, including a dyspeptic legion of economic hired guns, seem hell bent to prove otherwise. The natural counter balance for capitalist irrationality is unions. That's not to say that in some other epoch that unions will or have not been irrational in their demands, it's just that the balance of economic power has so shifted to capital that unions are, once again, a countervailing force that is prudent and necessary."

Nouriel Roubini, chairman of Roubini Global Economics, professor of economics at the Stern School of Business, New York University, and co-author of the book *Crisis Economics*, writes, "Mediocre income growth for everyone but the rich in the last few decades opened a gap between incomes and spending aspirations," which led to the

downturn in which businesses in the advanced economies of the world were cutting jobs because of inadequate demand leading to excess capacity. Cutting jobs weakens demand and weakens the economy further.

"The problem is not new," writes Roubini. "Karl Marx oversold socialism, but he was right in claiming that globalization, unfettered financial capitalism, and redistribution of income and wealth from labor to capital could lead capitalism to self-destruct. As he argued, unregulated capitalism can lead to regular bouts of over-capacity, under-consumption, and the recurrence of destructive financial crises, fueled by credit bubbles and asset-price booms and busts. Even before the Great Depression, Europe's enlightened 'bourgeois' classes recognized that, to avoid revolution, workers' rights needed to be protected, wage and labor conditions improved, and a welfare state created to redistribute wealth and finance public goods—education, health care, and a social safety net. The push towards a modern welfare state accelerated after the Great Depression, when the state took on the responsibility for macroeconomic stabilization—a role that required the maintenance of a large middle class by widening the provision of public goods through progressive taxation of incomes and wealth and fostering economic opportunity for all."

The rise of the social-welfare state was a response of market-oriented liberal democracies to the threat of popular revolutions, socialism, and communism that would recur during the periodic severe depressions of unregulated capitalism.

After regulations on the financial industries were instituted under President Franklin Roosevelt, the cruel boom-and-bust cycles of laissez-faire capitalism were somewhat tamed. Although the Supreme Court and conservative forces in the country blocked many of Roosevelt's initiatives to spur the economy, World War II ushered in a war economy. America had no arms industry. Roosevelt told the car manufacturers, you're going to make tanks now. It was the opposite of a laissez-faire, hands off free market, it was a command economy. But as a side effect of mounting a war effort, the economy was churned into productivity that produced a high standard of living in America in the post World War II years. From the late 1940s to the mid-1970s the U.S. enjoyed a period of relative calm in regard to the cruel boom and bust cycles that plagued capitalism of the previous two centuries.

Margaret Thatcher & Ronald Reagan

That cycle too played out and then came the 1980s and the rise of Reagan-Thatcher conservatism with its determination to slash regulation everywhere that it might hamper the profit seeking enterprises. It was a reaction to the excesses and failures of a bloated welfare state in Europe, which led, according to Roubini, to "yawning fiscal deficits, regulatory overkill, and a lack of economic dynamism that led to sclerotic growth then and the eurozone's sovereign-debt crisis now."

Thatcher went so far as to deny the very existence of society. On October 31, 1987, in an interview with Women's Own magazine, Thatcher said, "I think we've been through a period where too many people have been given to understand that if they have a problem, it's the government's job to cope with it. 'I have a problem, I'll get a grant.' 'I'm homeless, the government must house me.'

They're casting their problem on society. *And, you know, there is no such thing as society.* There are individual men and women, and there are families. And no government can do anything except through people, and people must look to themselves first. It's our duty to look after ourselves and then, also to look after our neighbor. People have got the entitlements too much in mind, without the obligations. There's no such thing as entitlement, unless someone has first met an obligation." [Italics added]

Now at the dawn of the 21st Century, the pendulum has swung back to the other extreme, and the underlying principles of the Reagan/Thatcher revolution have become dead dogma, an empty ideology that no longer addresses the problems of contemporary society.

Thirty years after the advent of Reaganism, Roubini says, the "laissez-faire Anglo-Saxon model has also now failed miserably. To stabilize market-oriented economies requires a return to the right balance between markets and provision of public goods. That means moving away from both the Anglo-Saxon model of unregulated markets and the continental European model of deficit-driven welfare states."

According to Roubini, this is a very serious problem. "Any economic model that does not properly address inequality will eventually face a crisis of legitimacy. Unless the relative economic roles of the market and the state are rebalanced, the protests of 2011 will become more severe, with social and political instability eventually harming long-term economic growth and welfare."

Unions help protect the economic security of the middle class and protect the big capitalists against their own excesses.

Natural Enemies: Unions and Fascism

Unions are the natural enemy of fascism. Oppositions to unions is one of the primary defining characteristics of fascism. Dr. Lawrence Britt, who studied the fascist regimes of Hitler (Germany), Mussolini (Italy), Franco (Spain), Suharto (Indonesia) and several

Latin American regimes, found 14 defining characteristics common to all of them. Number 10 in that list says that under fascist regimes, "Labor Power is Suppressed - Because the organizing power of labor is the only real threat to a fascist government, labor unions are either eliminated entirely, or are severely suppressed."

Remember, the creator of the first fascist state, Benito Mussolini, said, "Fascism might well be called corporatism because it is the merging of corporate and state power." Fascism is the takeover of government by corporate power. Unions are the "only real threat to a fascist government." Get the picture?

According to Bertram Gross, in *Friendly Fascism,* "In their march to power in Germany, Italy, and Japan the classic fascists were not stupid enough to concentrate on subverting the democratic machinery alone. They aimed their main attack, rather, against the non-government organizations most active in using and improving that machinery: namely, the labor movement and the political parties rooted in it. In Germany, where these organizations seemed immensely powerful, many German leaders thought that even with Adolf Hitler as chancellor, fascism could

make little headway. They underestimated the Nazis and their Big Business backers. 'All at once,' observed Karl Polanyi, the historian, 'the tremendous industrial and political organizations of labor and other devoted upholders of constitutional freedom would melt away and minute fascist forces would brush aside what seemed until then the overwhelming strength of democratic governments, parties and trade unions.'"

But even authoritarian states rely, in the end, on some measure of consent from the governed, or at least a belief in their legitimacy. According to Willis Harman in the book *Global Mind Change*, "Throughout history, the really fundamental changes in societies have come about not from dictates of governments and the results of battles but through vast numbers of people changing their minds —sometimes only a little bit. Some of the changes have amounted to profound transformations—for instance the transition from the Roman Empire to Medieval Europe, or from the Middle Ages to modern times. Others have been more specific, such as the constitution of democratic governments in England and America, or the termination of slavery as an accepted institution. In the latter cases, it is largely a matter of people recalling that no matter how powerful the economic or political or even military institution it persists because it has legitimacy, and that legitimacy comes from the perceptions of people. People give legitimacy and they can take it away. A challenge to legitimacy is probably the most powerful force for change to be found in history."

Unions as the Mirror of Corporate Power

The rise of organized labor mirrors the growth of corporate capitalism. Labor unions grew up in response to the rise and consolidation of ever larger corporate entities. Unions are a natural counterbalance, a countervailing force to the growth of corporate power. Ironically, unions are necessary for the success of capitalism. They protect capitalism from its own tendency to excess. Unions help protect democracy from capitalism run amuck. Unions are a force against the unhealthy concentration of capital and corporate power. Unions are one of the forces in society that help keep capitalism from evolving into fascism.

As corporate power becomes more concentrated and corporations pursue their mandate to maximize shareholder value, it is natural that they overstep the bounds of what is in the best interests of their employees and the communities they do business in. Quite simply, those interests do not appear on the corporate balance sheet.

In the system of thinking in which corporations exist only for maximizing profit, employees are seen as an expense, not a participant, and not entitled to a share in the fruits of the operation. Keeping expenses down is part of the mandate of a corporation. It must hold employee compensation down in order to push shareholder value up. That leaves the workers to fend for themselves. One worker versus a large corporation is not much of a match. But if all the workers join together, they can bring greater leverage to the negotiation. Whether it's the underlying threat of a work stoppage, or just the fact that it is in a company's best interests to respect and cultivate its human resources, an organization that represents a large number of people is stronger than an individual. When corporations in pursuit of profits push their prerogatives to the point that their employees feel cheated or abused, their employees begin to join forces to find ways to address their grievances.

The threat of corporations consolidating too much power was not lost on the early American leaders. Thomas Jefferson wrote, "I hope we shall crush... in its birth the aristocracy of our moneyed corporations, which dare already to challenge our government to a trial of strength and bid defiance to the laws of our country." This of course did not happen.

By the end of the Civil War, President Abraham Lincoln saw the rise of corporate power as a grave threat. On November 21, 1864, he wrote in a letter to Col. William F. Elkins, "We may congratulate ourselves that this cruel war is nearing its end. It has cost a vast amount of treasure and blood ... It has indeed been a trying hour for the Republic; but I see in the near future a crisis approaching that unnerves me and causes me to tremble for the safety of my country. As a result of the war, corporations have been enthroned and an era of corruption in high places will follow, and the money power of the country will endeavor to prolong its reign by working upon the prejudices of the people until all wealth is aggregated in a few hands and the Republic is destroyed. I feel at this moment more anxiety for the safety of my country than ever before, even in the midst of war. God grant that my suspicions may prove groundless."

Abraham Lincoln

In 1888, President Grover Cleveland said, "As we view the achievements of aggregated capital, we discover the existence of trusts, combinations, and monopolies, while the citizen is struggling far in the rear or is trampled to death beneath an iron heel. Corporations, which should be the carefully restrained creatures of the law and the servants of the people, are fast becoming the people's masters."

Franklin D. Roosevelt, in an April 29, 1938, message to Congress, warned that the growth of private power could lead to fascism. "The liberty of a democracy is not safe if the people tolerate the growth of private power to a point where it becomes stronger than their democratic state itself," he said. "That, in its essence, is fascism—ownership of government by an individual, by a group, or by any other controlling private power."

In his Farewell Address, his last message to the people as president, Dwight D. Eisenhower warned of unwarranted influence of a group of business interests based on war. He called that network of companies the military industrial complex.

The 20th Century, then only half over, had already seen three major wars that involved the U.S. That necessitated the creation of a permanent arms industry, Eisenhower said, which was unprecedented in America. "Until the latest of our world conflicts, the United States had no armaments industry..." he said. "This conjunction of an immense military establishment and a large arms industry is new in the American experience. The total influence—economic, political, even spiritual—is felt in every city, every Statehouse, every office of the Federal government. We recognize the imperative need for this development. Yet we must not fail to comprehend its grave implications. Our toil, resources and livelihood are all involved; so is the very structure of our society. In the councils of government, we must guard against the acquisition of unwarranted influence, whether sought or unsought, by the military-industrial complex. The potential for the disastrous rise of misplaced power exists and will persist."

Corporate Propaganda: The Hidden Manipulators

According to Alex Carey, an Australian social psychologist who studied corporate propaganda, "The twentieth century has been characterized by three developments of great political importance: the growth of democracy, the growth of corporate power, and the growth of corporate propaganda as a means of protecting corporate power against democracy."

According to Noam Chomsky,

"That the growth of corporate power would undermine freedom and democracy had been understood by classical liberal opinion well before the contours of the future industrial capitalist society could be clearly discerned. In his later years Thomas Jefferson warned that the newly rising 'banking institutions and moneyed incorporations' would destroy the freedoms won in the American revolution, becoming the foundation of a 'single and splendid government of aristocracy.'"

Noam Chomsky

Corporate law was shaped by the elite for the elite, not by expression of popular will through legislative processes, but by courts and lawyers acting in "technocratic insulation" from the public, as the World Bank describes its own recommended modus operandi.

This kind of behavior from self-appointed rulers of society has a long history, rooted in aristocratic traditions dating back to feudal times and farther. According to Chomsky, "At the time of the first modern democratic revolution in 17th Century England, the self-described 'men of best quality' expressed concern that the 'rascal multitude' might seek to enter the public arena, aroused by pamphleteers, itinerant preachers and other riffraff who had 'made the people thereby so curious and so arrogant that they will never find humility enough to submit to a civil rule.'"

The Power of the Propaganda System

Few people are aware of the extent to which their thoughts and the thoughts of others are influenced by propaganda, that is, messages that are devised primarily for the purposes of persuasion. Often the messages transmitted through propaganda are transmitted subliminally, hidden under the overt message. The corporate elite is an aristocracy made up of the wealthiest corporations, which established themselves consciously and deliberately as a modern aristocracy. In a democratic society, where physical coercion was limited by law and custom, propaganda became the best way to control masses of people.

The class of people groomed to believe that they are born to be the rulers take whatever action they see as necessary to ensure that they remain in control. In Jack London's *The Iron Heel* he describes the ruling Oligarchy. "They, as a class, believed that they alone maintained civilization. It was their belief that if ever they weakened, the great beast would engulf them and everything of beauty and wonder and joy and good in its cavernous and slime-dripping maw. Without them, anarchy would reign and humanity would drop backward into the primitive night out of which it had so painfully emerged."

One of the means by which self-appointed rulers maintain control of their subjects is by the use of propaganda. Theories of persuasion date back at least as far as 500 B.C. in Greece. But with the emergence of an industrial society with mass communications, many new possibilities were opened in the art of mass persuasion. In the 20th Century techniques of propaganda developed a degree of sophistication never seen before. Persuasion and manipulation became a science. "Consumers" were studied scientifically in terms of what they wanted, and what kind of symbols and techniques of persuasion they would respond to. With the coming of the first World War, the new techniques of mass propaganda were explored for the first time to rally people to the cause, to engender hate for the people targeted as The Enemy, and sympathy for those who were to be allies. For the first time mass propaganda became a central tool of politics and war. As Noam Chomsky has pointed out, propaganda is even more important in democratic societies than in authoritarian societies, where brute force can be used openly to suppress dissent and manage societies. As the techniques of wartime propaganda were adapted to peacetime use, the practices became known as public relations.

Propaganda in a Democratic Society

Although we are taught in school that we live in a democratic country ruled by the will of the people, according to Noam Chomsky, propaganda is even more important to the dominant forces in a free society than in an autocratic society. Since the power elite of a free society cannot freely use naked force to make the people comply, it is important to use persuasion to make people comply voluntarily. In a dictatorship, it doesn't matter as much what people think, because they can be forced to obey.

Robert Brady, who studied corporate propaganda in 1943, said, "The importance of public relations ... decreases as one moves away from countries with long and deep-seated liberal, democratic and parliamentary institutions." Italy and Japan had the most primitive propaganda. Germany, which had more of a democratic tradition, had propaganda that was "better organized ... more vociferous and more versatile." ...

And the countries with the longest experience of liberal, democratic institutions have always had the most sophisticated, subtle and effective propaganda. The country with the most effective, nuanced and ubiquitous techniques of subliminal persuasion is the United States. Turning on TV in America, one is immediately sucked into a world of enchantment, a fantasy more vivid and dazzling than reality. Millions of dollars are invested in a one-minute commercial, and the advertisers keep paying it because they get their money's worth. Advertising and public relations sell products and services, and political candidates, but underlying those specific objects, they also sell a world view, an ideology that supports the corporate consumer society.

The Development of Modern Propaganda

The father of modern propaganda and of the public relations industry was Edward Bernays, the nephew of Sigmund Freud. Bernays worked for the U.S. government's propaganda operation in World War I. There were many German Americans and there were few clear reasons why America should choose to go to side with the British and French instead of the Germans. A propaganda campaign was launched to stir up hatred and fear of the Germans, calling them "the Huns." They went so far as to show false stories of Hessian soldiers bayoneting babies.

It's hard for historians today to state a justification for World War I. Jack London's portrayal of the push toward war in his fictional *The Iron Heel* shows the side of war that doesn't usually appear in the newspapers. "The Oligarchy wanted the war with Germany. And it wanted the war for a dozen reasons. In the juggling of events such a war would cause, in the reshuffling of international cards and the making of new treaties and alliances, the Oligarchy had much to gain. And furthermore, the war would consume many national surpluses, reduce the armies of unemployed that menaced all countries, and give the Oligarchy a breathing space in which to perfect its plans and carry them out. Such a war would virtually put the Oligarchy in possession of the world market. Also, such a war would create a large standing army that need never be disbanded, while in the minds of the people would be substituted the issue 'America versus Germany,' in place of 'Socialism versus Oligarchy.'"

The propaganda effort succeeded to the extent that the U.S. did go to war against Germany. Even today few people can come up with a coherent reason for why that war had to be fought, or what was accomplished by the millions of deaths, the massive destruction and misery that resulted from the war. But some of the family fortunes built on the war are probably still intact.

Bernays and the Creation of the PR Industry

After World War I ended, Bernays, who had perfected the U.S. war propaganda machine, turned his efforts to peacetime. Bernays saw the power of information and persuasion during the war. It was, he said, "the first time the U.S. used ideas as weapons of war." And, he reasoned that "If this could be used for war, it can be used for peace."

He founded the first PR firm in 1919. His efforts helped to bring about the building of Route 66, a transcontinental highway that was the forerunner of the interstate highway system. His client, Mack Trucks, wanted the taxpayer to fund roads to help its business.

He also helped to win over women for the tobacco industry, helping to make smoking an acceptable practice for women. Bernays created fashion magazine spreads showing stylish models holding cigarettes. The New York Times and papers across the country ran front page photos of women smokers marching in the 1934 New York Easter Parade.

The new practice of public relations found favor and rapidly spread throughout corporate America. It was, after all tax deductible. Money spent on PR, as a business expense, is not taxed, which in fact creates an indirect public subsidy on the practice.

The PR War on Unions

In the battle between corporate power and union resistance, propaganda has played and continues to play a key role. At the onset of the 21st Century, the world view of Americans is largely shaped by Corporate propaganda, including the public's view of unions, what they are and what they mean to American history and the quality of life of Americans.

Alex Carey, an Australian scholar to whom Noam Chomsky gives credit for the pioneering research that led to Chomsky's *Manufacturing Consent, said,* "The twentieth century has been characterized by three developments of great political importance: the growth of democracy, the growth of corporate power, and the growth of corporate propaganda as a means of protecting corporate power against democracy."

To Carey, the role of unions in this dynamic is central. "There have been two principal aspects to the growth of democracy in this century," Carey says, "the extension of the franchise (i.e. the right to vote) and the growth of the union movement. These developments have presented corporations with potential threats to their power from the people at large (i.e. from public opinion) and from organized labor. American corporations have met this threat by learning to use propaganda, both inside and outside the corporation, as an effective weapon for managing governments and public opinion. They have thereby been able to subordinate the expression of democratic aspirations and the interests of larger public purposes to their own narrow corporate purposes."

Carey defines propaganda as "communications where the form and content is selected with the single-minded purpose of bringing some target audience to adopt the attitudes and beliefs chosen in advance by the sponsors of the communications."

Corporate propaganda, or what is known as corporate communications, is targeted in two directions: within, to employees of the corporation, and without, to the public at large. That which is focused on the public has two objectives. One is to identify the free market system in popular consciousness with every cherished value of the culture. The other is to identify the adversaries of corporate power with "tyranny, oppression and even subversion." The adversaries the corporate state recognizes and targets are "interventionist governments and strong unions (the only agencies capable of checking the complete domination of society by the corporations)."

According to Carey, corporations direct propaganda to employees that is designed to undermine their relationships with and their confidence in their unions. The techniques used are deceptively titled "human relations", "employee participation" and "employee communications." From the beginning of the 20th Century American businesses have mounted large scale, professionally coordinated propaganda campaigns. The widespread use of these techniques over a long period has brought into being a large complex of institutions that are involved in this process, specializing in social research and propaganda. This amounts to what Carey calls a 75-year multi-billion dollar social engineering project on a national scale. For 50 years U.S. businesses refined and perfected these practices and in the 1970s the practices started moving overseas to other countries.

In the 1930s and 1940s, Carey says, the battleground between corporations and unions shifted from the field of direct action and picket line organizing to the field of public opinion using the weapons of mass media. In this realm corporations had a great advantage because of their superior resources and capital. The expert skills of public relations went to work undermining the public opinion about unions. The turning point was the Steel Strike of 1919.

Propaganda and the Steel Strike of 1919

The corporatocracy's first test of business employing propaganda as a peacetime weapon, public relations, came in 1919. "At the outset, public opinion favored the strikers, who worked 84-hour

weeks under notoriously bad conditions," said Carey. But five days after the strike began, the Steel Corporation launched a campaign with full-page ads urging strikers to return to work, saying union leaders were "trying to establish the red rule of anarchy and bolshevism," that the strike was "un-American" and that "the Huns had a hand in fomenting the strike." The Huns were the current villain in mass propaganda and the idea of the Germans as the enemy had already been driven hard by tremendous war propaganda campaigns.

The strike was monitored by the Interchurch World Movement (IWM), which was made up of 26 Protestant churches. The organization produced a two-volume report that said that the strike was defeated by "the strike breaking methods of the Steel companies and their effective mobilization of public opinion against the strikers through charges of radicalism, bolshevism and the closed shop, none of which were justified by the facts" and through "the hostility of the press giving biased and colored news." According to historian Robert Murray, "When the strike ended in 1920 the men had gained not a single concession ... 20 lives had been sacrificed and ... $112 million ... lost in wages. Backed by a favorable public opinion which was based on an exaggerated fear of bolshevism, this corporation proved that not even 350,000 striking workers could prevail against it."

It was a turning point. The battle for power between corporations and unions had shifted. When legislation had proven ineffective against unfair labor practices, unions had moved to collective bargaining, direct action. But the breaking of the steel strike in 1920 proved that those methods had now been rendered ineffective by more sophisticated techniques of propaganda employed by the corporations.

Mightier than the Sword

In 1935 when the U.S. government got around to recognizing some rights of working people, the corporate world put aside physical force and turned to propaganda and public relations to achieve its ends.

"Beginning in 1945," Carey said, "the post-war conservative assault on public opinion revived the two dominant themes of the 1930s: (1) Identification of the traditional American free enterprise system with social harmony, freedom, democracy, family, church and patriotism, and (2) identification of all government regulation of affairs of business, and all liberals who supported such interference, with communism and subversion."

Chapter Two:

Timeline of the American Labor Movement

The history of unions and the labor movement in America is the story of a vast social movement, made up of countless individual stories, struggles rising up separately in communities across the country. The history of labor is diverse, made up of a broad and varied tapestry of events that could fill many volumes. So before dropping down to look at some of its major events close up, here is a bird's eye view in the form of a timeline to give an overview of that history and the rocky progression of the labor movement.

1823
Hatters in New York City are tried for going on strike and convicted of conspiracy.

1825
Carpenters in Boston become the first to strike for the 10-hour work day.

1797
Profit sharing introduced at Albert Gallatin's glass works in New Geneva, Pennsylvania.

1831
Nat Turner leads a slave rebellion in Virginia. He is captured and executed.

1838
One-third of the nation's workers become unemployed in the recession following the Panic of 1837.

1827
Tailors in Philadelphia go on strike to protest the firing of fellow workers who asked for a raise. They were tried for conspiracy and convicted with the verdict citing "injury to trade."

1837
The Panic of 1837 destroys the National Trades Union and most other unions. President Andrew Jackson declares the ten-hour day in the Philadelphia Navy Yard to quell discontent caused by Panic of 1837.

1835
Children working at the silk mills in Patterson, New Jersey, go on strike for an 11-hour day and six-day week.

The first federal government employee work stoppage begins when workers at the Washington and Philadelphia Navy yards launch the first strike of federal employees when they strike for a 10-hour day and a redress of their grievances.

1806
The Union of Philadelphia Journeymen Cordwainers become the first union to be tried and convicted of criminal conspiracy for striking for higher wages. The fines they were forced to pay bankrupted the union and forced it to disband.

1800
Strikers are found guilty of conspiracy for trying to bargain collectively to get a pay raise in the case Commonwealth v Pullis.

1619
North America's first recorded labor uprising takes place in Jamestown, Virginia, when Polish craftsmen, who produced tar, pitch and glass, strike to protest their lack of voting rights. It ended peacefully when the workers were granted full voting rights.

1840
President Martin Van Buren proclaims the 10-hour-work day without reduction in pay for federal employees on public works.

1842
The Massachusetts Supreme Court rules in the case Commonwealth v. Hunt that labor unions are not in themselves illegal conspiracies and that workers have the right to organize and strike for better wages.

Connecticut and Massachusetts pass laws prohibiting children from working more than a 10-hour-work day.

1848
An anti-child labor law is passed in Pennsylvania making the minimum 12 years age for workers in commercial occupations.

Pennsylvania passes a 10-hour day law. When employers violate the new law, women mill workers riot and attack the factory gates with axes.

1850
The Compromise of 1850 perpetuates slavery.

1851
Two railroad strikers are shot and killed and many others are injured by the state militia in Portage, New York.

1860
Shoemakers in Lynn, Massachusetts go on strike with 800 women operatives and 4,000 workmen marching. Abraham Lincoln supports the shoemakers, saying, "Thank God that we have a system of labor where there can be a strike."

1863
Lincoln issued the Emancipation Proclamation which frees slaves in the southern areas that Union forces occupied.

The first railroad labor union, The Brotherhood of the Footboard (later renamed the Brotherhood of Locomotive Engineers) is formed in Marshall, Michigan.

1864
The legality of importing immigrants by holding a portion of their wages or property is upheld in the Contract Labor Law. The practice was outlawed with the Foran Act of 1885.

1865
The 13th Amendment to the Constitution bans slavery in US.

1866
The National Labor Union is formed, the first national labor federation in the US.

1867
Chicago trade unions hold a general strike demanding an eight-hour day.

1868
The federal government establishes the eight-hour work day for government employees.

1869
The Black National Labor Union was founded in Washington DC under the leadership of Isaak Myers.

Seven members of the Philadelphia tailors' union, led by Uriah Smith Stephens and James L. Wright, organize a new secret union known as the The Noble Order of the Knights of Labor in Philadelphia.

Daughters of St. Crispin, the first national female union is organized with a convention in Lynn, Massachusetts, that elects Carrie Wilson president.

1870
Coal miners and coal mine operators signed the first written labor contract.

1870 (con't)
Battle of Viaduct - The Great Railroad Strike was a general strike to protest a cut in wages in which federal troops were called in. Thirty workers were killed during the protest.

1873
The Panic of 1873 sets off an economic slump that wipes out most national unions.

The Brotherhood of Locomotive Firemen was established. In 1906 it became the Brotherhood of Locomotive Firemen & Enginemen.

1874 (1870?)
Unemployed workers demonstrate in Tompkins Square Park in New York City. Mounted police charge into the crowd, beating men, women and children with billy clubs and causing hundreds of casualties. Police Commissioner, Abram Duryee, says, "It was the most glorious sight I ever saw..." New York City police injure dozens of unemployed people at a rally.

1886
In Columbus, Ohio, a group of workers under the leadership of Samuel Gompers form the American Federation of Labor.

Hundreds of thousands of American workers protest to demand the eight-hour day. Chicago manufacturing was brought to a standstill. At the McCormick Reaper factory a battle broke out between locked-out union workers and the non-unionist workers. Heavily armed Chicago Police move in with clubs and guns, leaving four union workers dead and many others wounded.

1877
On June 21, 10 coal-mining activists known as Molly Maguires are hanged in Pennsylvania.

On July 14 a railroad strike spreads state to state, bringing railroad traffic nationally practically to a halt. Some state militias side with strikers, so federal troops are called out to stop the strikes. At the Battle of the Viaduct in Chicago, federal troops who had recently returned from an Indian massacre killed 30 workers and wounded more than 100.

1882
The First Labor Day celebration was held in New York City with 30,000 workers marching in a parade.

1884
The Federal Bureau of Labor established as part of Department of the Interior.

The Federation of Organized Trades and Labor Unions, a forerunner of the AFL, passed a resolution stating that "eight hours shall constitute a legal day's work from and after May 1, 1886." Though the Federation did not intend to stimulate a mass insurgency, its resolution had precisely that effect.

1885
The Foran Act outlaws immigration of laborers on contract.

Fourteen coal mining activists are hung in Pennsylvania (Molly Maguires).

Hundreds of thousands of workers join the young labor organization the Knights of Labor. Early the next year they will take to the streets to demand the eight-hour day.

1886 (con't)

At Haymarket Square in Chicago a rally in support of the eight-hour day becomes a riot after an explosion kills several people, including policemen, and injures 67 others. In the ensuing hysteria city and state government officials rounded up eight anarchists, tried them for murder, and sentenced them to death. Later, the incident becomes the basis of May Day celebrations in honor of labor.

In the Great Southwest Railroad Strike 200,000 employees of the Pacific and Missouri Pacific railroads go on strike. Pinkerton detectives are called in to beat strikers. Missouri and Texas bring in state militias.

In the Bay View Massacre, 2,000 Polish workers go on strike in Milwaukee to call for an eight-hour day. Workers from other factories joined them. All but one factory is closed down and 16,000 protestors gathered at Rolling Hills. The governor calls up the state militia and orders them to fire on the crowd, which they do, killing seven people, including a child. The Milwaukee Journal reported that eight more would die within 24 hours, and commended the governor for his quick action.

1887

On November 11, four of the eight anarchists accused in the Haymarket Square explosion are executed, including anarchist leaders August Spies and Albert Parsons. Though they had been on the record advocating armed struggle, there was no evidence any of them had been involved in the throwing of the bomb. A quarter of a million people lined Chicago's street during a funeral procession for one of the executed strikers to express outrage. Haymarket became a symbol of inequality and injustice.

In Thibodaux, Louisiana, the Louisiana state militia, joined by bands of civilians, shot 35 unarmed black sugar workers who were striking for a dollar-a-day wage. The authorities also lynched two of the strike's leaders.

1890

Eugene V. Debs founds the American Railway Union (ARU) as an all craft organization.

After a seven-month strike New York garment workers win the right to unionize, a closed shop, and the dismissal of scabs.

1894

21 April – June 1894 (United States) Bituminous Coal Miners' Strike of 1894 — Miners of hard coal in the United States stage a two-month nation-wide strike known as Bituminous Coal Miners' Strike. The strike was unsuccessful and led almost to the destruction of the United Mine Workers union.

1893

The first of several bloody mining strikes takes place at Cripple Creek, Colorado.

Workers went on strike against the Pullman Palace Car Company in protest of a pay cut, and during the strike the 1892 World's Columbian Exposition in Chicago's Jackson Park was set on fire, with seven buildings destroyed. The mob continued burning and looting railroad cars and fighting police until 14,000 federal and state troops moved in to stop the strike.

Unions help win the passage of the Safety Appliance Act, which outlaws some dangerous equipment used by railroad companies.

1892

During the Homestead Strike in Homestead, Pennsylvania, Pinkerton guards fire on striking Carnegie mill steel workers. Seven guards and 11 strikers and bystanders were shot to death.

The Amalgamated Association of Iron, Steel, and Tin Workers lose the fight over Carnegie Steel's attempt to break the union.

Miners on strike in Coeur D'Alene, Idaho, dynamite the Frisco Mill, destroying it.

1894 (con't)
A strike by American Railway Union workers led by Eugene Debs against the Pullman Palace Car Company near Chicago was defeated by injunctions and 14,000 federal troops, who killed 34 American Railway Union members. Debs and several others were imprisoned for violating injunctions and the union fell apart.

1897
On September 10 near Lattimer, Pennsylvania, nine unarmed striking coal miners and mine workers were killed and 36 wounded by a posse organized by the Luzerne County sheriff. The strikers had been brought in as strike-breakers, but later organized themselves in protest. Most of those who died were shot in the back.

1899
Members of the Western Federation of Miners dynamited the mill of the Bunker Hill Company at Wardner, Idaho, destroying it. President McKinley sent in black soldiers from Brownsville, Texas, who rounded up thousands of miners and imprisoned them in bullpens.

U.S. Army Troops occupied the Coeur d'Alene mining region in Idaho through 1901.

1903
The Department of Commerce and Labor is established.

Troops are sent into Cripple Creek, Colorado, to control rioting by striking coal miners.

Organizer Mother Jones (Mary Harris Jones) leads the March of the Mill Children to President Roosevelt's home in New York as part of efforts to demand a 55-hour work week. Many of the children were victims of industrial accidents.

1905
The Supreme Court rules that a law limiting the number of hours New York bakery workers could work is unconstitutional under the due process clause of the 14th amendment.

1904
William Randolph Hearst's San Francisco Chronicle begins publishing articles railing against Japanese immigrant laborers. The California Legislature passes a resolution declaring that action should be taken against Japanese immigration.

A battle breaks out between the Colorado Militia and striking miners at Dunnville. Six union members are killed, 15 taken prisoner and 79 strikers deported to Kansas.

1902
Fourteen strikers at an anthracite coal mine in Pana, Illinois, are killed and 22 wounded by scabherders. President Theodore Roosevelt, concerned about a coal shortage for the winter, becomes the first president to step in to help negotiate a strike settlement, appointing a commission to arbitrate negotiations between miners and owners. Miners ended up with a 10 percent raise and a shortened work day.

1898
Part of the Erdman Act, which made it a criminal offense for railroads to dismiss employees or discriminate against prospective employees based on union activities, was declared invalid by the U.S. Supreme Court.

On October 12, 14 were killed and 25 wounded in violence resulting when Virden, Illinois mine owners attempted to break a strike by importing 200 non-union black workers.

1896
On September 21, the state militia was sent into Leadville, Colorado, to crack down on a miner's strike.

1906

Upton Sinclair publishes his novel *The Jungle*, vividly portraying the unsafe and unclean practices of the Chicago meat-packing industry. The novel raises awareness of working conditions.

1908

Section 10 of the Erdman Act, which prohibited railroad corporations from firing employees for being members of unions, was declared unconstitutional.

The Federal Employers' Liability Act was passed, helping to hold railroads responsible for injuries caused by unsafe equipment.

1911

The Supreme Court ordered the American Federation of Labor to stop supporting a boycott against the Bucks Stove and Range Company, affirming a lower court order. A contempt charge is filed against union leaders, including AFL President Samuel Gompers. In a second contempt trial a year later three AFL leaders are sentenced to prison but the Supreme Court overturned it based on a three-year statute of limitations.

A fire broke out at the Triangle Shirtwaist Company that was housed in the top three floors of a 10-story building in New York, killing 147 people, most of them women and girls who worked in sweatshop conditions. Fifty of them died from leaping from the windows to escape the fire. Some were trampled, others burned to death, and many were prevented from escaping because of locked stairway exits used to control and confine workers. The company's owners were indicted for manslaughter and the incident led to the establishment of the New York Factory Investigating Commission to monitor factory conditions.

Labor unions paid a Chicago "slugger" $50 for every scab he discouraged by slugging them.

1912

A textile strike took place in Lawrence, Massachusetts, known as the Bread and Roses strike because it is said that women carried signs saying, "We want bread, but we want roses too." The action was led primarily by women workers. Many different immigrant communities joined forces with the support of the Industrial Workers of the World. The strike is known for originating the moving picket line, a tactic designed to avoid strikers being charged with loitering. The strike lasted two months, was considered successful, winning a pay increase, time-and-a-quarter pay for overtime, and a promise of no discrimination against strikers.

The Boiler Act is passed, later evolving into the Locomotive Inspection Act. It required railroad companies to keep their equipment in safe working order and to be able to pass inspections.

1910

During a strike at the Llewellyn Ironworks in Los Angeles, a dynamite bomb destroyed part of the factory.

The 1910 Accident Reports Act is passed, furthering on the gains made with the Federal Employers' Liability Act two years before.

The Railway Brotherhoods win a 10-hour work day and standardization of rates of pay and working conditions from the railroad companies.

On October 1, the Los Angeles Times building is bombed, destroying the building and killing 20 people. The paper's owner blames the fire on the unions. The unions deny the charge.

1909

Female garment workers in New York go on strike in the Uprising of the 20,000, resulting in many of them being arrested.

1912 (con't)

The National Guard is called out against striking West Virginia coal miners.

Members of The Brotherhood of Timber Workers go on strike and workers and their supporters become involved in an armed confrontation with the Galloway Lumber Company and its supporters in what was called the Grabow Riot. Four died and 40 to 50 were wounded.

1914

Ford raises its starting wage from $2.40 for a nine hour day to $5 for an eight hour day.

John D. Rockefeller, Jr. and other mine owners hired guards to oppose strikers against the Colorado Fuel and Iron Company at Colorado's Ludlow Mine Field. The guards attacked a union tent camp with machine guns and set it on fire, killing five men, two women, and 12 children in what became known as the Ludlow Massacre.

The Clayton Act, limiting the use of injunctions in labor disputes is passed into law.

After an unsuccessful strike by the United Mine Workers, the President appointed the Colorado Coal Commission to investigate the Ludlow Massacre and labor conditions in the mines.

The militia in Butte, Montana, crush a strike by the Western Federation of Miners.

The Commission on Industrial Relations issues a report stating that approximately 35,000 workers were killed and 700,000 workers injured in industrial accidents in the U.S.

1916

Federal employees win the right to receive worker's compensation insurance.

Railroad workers win the eight-hour day with the passage of the Adamson Act, passed in time to avert a nationwide strike.

A Federal child labor law is enacted but later declared unconstitutional.

A bomb is set off during a Preparedness Day parade in San Francisco killing 10 and injuring 40 more. Labor organizer Thomas J. Mooney and Shoe Worker Warren K. Billings were convicted of first-degree and second-degree murder, respectively, then pardoned in 1939.

1915

Labor leader Joe Hill is arrested in Salt Lake City, convicted on phony murder charges and hanged 21 months later despite worldwide protests and two attempts of President Woodrow Wilson to intervene. In a letter to Bill Haywood shortly before his death, Joe Hill wrote words that became a mantra for labor: "Don't mourn - organize!"

Employees of the American Agricultural Chemical Company, the Consumer's Fertilizer Company and Armour and Company went on strike January 4 for a return to a $2-a-day wage that had been reduced to $1.60 a day. Consumer's Fertilizer met the demands. The others didn't. Armed guards were brought in from New York. They fired on the strikers, killing one and wounding 20.

The Supreme Court upholds the legality of "yellow dog" contracts, which forbid membership in labor unions.

1913

In a strike against the United Fruit Company in New Orleans, three maritime workers were shot and one killed by police.

The US Department of Labor is established. Secretary of Labor was given the power to "act as a mediator and to appoint commissioners of conciliation in labor disputes."

1916 (con't)

The owner of Everett Mills, in Everett, Washington, hired strikebreakers who attacked and beat strikers while police watched, refusing to intervene because they said it was federal land and outside their jurisdiction. But when strikers fought back, police intervened, claiming that the picketers had crossed the line of jurisdiction. When union members tried to speak at a local crossroads, vigilantes captured them and subjected them to running the gauntlet (running through a line of soldiers while each is throwing blows), whipping, kicking and being impaled against a spiked cattle guard. Violence continued for months, with many killed, wounded or missing.

1917

Organizer Frank Little of The Industrial Workers of the World is lynched in Butte, Montana. Federal agents raid IWW headquarters in 48 cities.

At the copper mines in Bisbee, Arizona, Sheriff Harry Wheeler organized a deportation of 1,185 workers who had gone on strike for improvements to safety and working conditions, an end to discrimination against labor organizations, discrimination against foreign and minority workers, and for a fair wage system. Thousands of vigilantes forced the men into manure-covered boxcars and sent them to the New Mexico desert.

1918

United Mine Workers Organizer Ginger Goodwin is shot by a hired police officer near Cumberland, British Colombia.

1920

The U.S. Bureau of Investigation launched a nationwide assault against labor in a campaign that became known as the Palmer Raids, in which agents seized labor leaders and literature. Some were turned over to state officials for prosecution under anti-anarchy statutes.

The women's suffrage amendment was ratified.

In Matewan, West Virginia, the local mining company and 13 company managers hired Baldwin-Felts detectives to evict miners and their families from the Stone Mountain Mine camp, leading to what became known as the Battle of Matewan. The police chief, a former miner, and the mayor tried to protect the miners in their union drive, but a gun battle left seven detectives, the mayor and two strikers dead. Fifteen months later Baldwin-Felts detectives assassinated the police chief, setting off an armed rebellion of 10,000 West Virgina coal miners at The Battle of Blair Mountain. Army troops intervened. The battle has been called the largest insurrection in America since the Civil War.

1919

Company guards shoot United Mine Worker organizer Fannie Sellins dead in Brackenridge, Pennsylvania.

Looting and rioting break out in Boston after 1,117 Boston policemen declared a work stoppage after failed attempts to affiliate with the American Federation of labor. Massachusetts Governor Calvin Coolidge called out the state militia to put down the strike.

Legionnaires attack a Centralia, Washington, IWW hall during an armistice day celebration. Four legionnaires were shot and killed by members of IWW, after which legionnaires lynched IWW organizer Wesley Everest.

In the Great Steel Strike, 350,000 steel workers walk off the job demanding recognition of their union. Three months later, the AFL Iron and Steel Organizing Committee call off the strike without achieving their goals. Two hundred fifty union activists are deported to Russia as the Red Scare takes hold in America.

1921
The Supreme Court ruled that the Clayton Act did not legalize secondary boycotts or protect unions against injunctions brought against them for conspiracy in restraint of trade. In Truax v. Corrigan, the Supreme Court ruled that an Arizona law allowing strikes and forbidding injunctions in labor disputes was unconstitutional under the 14th amendment.

1922
In the case Coronado Coal Co. v. UMMA the United Mine Workers was not held responsible for local strike action, which was ruled to be not a conspiracy to restrain trade within the Sherman Anti-Trust Act.

In Herrin, Illinois, three union miners are killed. In retaliation miners kill 20 guards and strikebreakers are killed in what became known as the Herrin Massacre.

1923
During a maritime strike in San Pedro, California, the IWW Union Hall is raided and demolished.

1924
AFL President Samuel Gompers dies. He is succeeded by William Green.

An amendment to the Constitution was proposed to restrict child labor, but only 28 states ratified it and 36 were required to make it law.

1925
Phillip Randolph joined with other porters to found The Brotherhood of Sleeping Car Porters, the first African American union. The Pullman Company called Randolph a communist and recruited middle class African American leaders to oppose the union on the grounds that organizers were troublemakers and their work was not in the best interests of African Americans.

The AFL supported Randolph's efforts, but still denied membership to African Americans, as did most other unions at the time.

1930
Labor racketeers known as the Chicagorillas shot and killed contractor William Healy, who had been engaged in struggles with the Chicago Marble Setters Union.

1929
The Hayes-Cooper Act regulating the shipment of prison labor goods in interstate commerce is signed into law.

The stock market crash in October sets off The Great Depression, the worst economic collapse in American history.

During the Loray Mill Strike in North Carolina the National Guard are called out to put down the strike.

1927
IWW coal miners are massacred while marching for better work conditions in Columbine mine massacre in the company town of Serene, Colorado.

1926
The Railway Labor Act required employers to enjoin in collective bargaining and not discriminate against union members. It also set up mediation and voluntary arbitration in labor disputes.

Textile workers fight with police in Passaic, New Jersey, in a strike that lasted a year.

Striking miners were massacred in Columbine, Colorado.

In Wheeling, West Virginia, labor racketeers blow up two Glendale Gas and Coal Company houses occupied by non-Union miners.

1930 (con't)
More than 100 farm workers were arrested for union organizing in Imperial Valley, California. Eight were convicted of "criminal syndicalism."

1931
Armed vigilantes attack striking miners in Harlan County, Kentucky.

Congress passes the Davis-Bacon Act, which mandates the payment of the prevailing wages to employees of contractors and subcontractors on public construction.

1932
The Anti-Injunction Act prohibits Federal injunctions in most labor disputes.

Wisconsin passes the first unemployment insurance act in the United States.

Police kill strikers at Ford's Dearborn, Michigan, plant.

1933
Eighteen thousand cotton pickers in Pixley, California, strike for a raise in pay and four are killed before the raise is granted.

1935
The Wagner Act, or National Labor Relations Act, sets the first national labor policy of protecting the right of workers to organize and elect representatives for collective bargaining. The law gave the Brotherhood of Sleeping Car Porters legal support in their dealings with the Pullman Company and helped to revive the African American union's sagging prospects.

1934
More than 500,000 millworkers walk off jobs in the Great Uprising of '34.

The Secretary of Labor convenes the first National Labor Legislation Conference to seek closer cooperation between federal and state governments in creating workable national labor legislation.

The US joined the International Labor Organization.

National Guardsmen kill two and wound more than 200 strikers in Toledo, Ohio, during the Electric Auto-Lite Strike.

In May police fire on striking Teamster truck drivers in Minneapolis who were demanding recognition of their union, wage increases, and shorter working hours. As violence escalates, the governor declares martial law in Minneapolis, deploying 4,000 National Guardsmen. The strike finally ends August 21 when company owners accept union demands.

In Woonsocket, Rhode Island, more than 420,000 textile workers strike as part of a national movement to win a minimum wage for textile workers. Three workers are killed.

San Francisco Police shoot and kill two longshoremen during the International Longshoreman's and Warehouse Union strike.

Three workers are killed in Woonsocket, Rhode Island, in a strike that was part of a national movement to win a fair minimum wage for textile workers. More than 420,000 workers join the strike.

A. Phillip Randolph begins speaking at AFL conventions calling for the integration of African Americans in the labor movement.

1935 (con't)
The Social Security Act is approved.

The Committee for Industrial Organization (CIO) is formed within the AFL to foster industrial unionism.

1937
After a sit-down strike General Motors recognizes the United Auto Workers union. But after succeeding in organizing GM and Chrysler, Walter Reuther and a group from the UAW tried to pass out leaflets at Ford Motor Company's River Rouge plant and were beaten by Ford guards.

Police kill 10 people and wound 80 in Southside Chicago during the "Little Steel" strikes by the Steel Workers Organizing Committee against Republic Steel in what became known as the Memorial Day Massacre. Police attacked an unarmed crowd of men and women who were supporting the strike. The strike continued for five weeks. It was finally broken when Inland Steel employees went back to work without achieving union recognition or other objectives.

The CIO was expelled from the AFL over charges of dual unionism or competition.

The Brotherhood of Sleeping Car Porters won its first contract from the Pullman Company, with a pay raise, a reduction in work hours, some job security, and the right to have union representation.

1939
The Supreme Court rules that sit-down strikes are illegal.

1941
The United States entered World War II on December 8. The AFL and the CIO announced a no-strike pledge for the duration of the war.

1945
World War II ended.

1940
In the Apex Hosiery Co. v. Leader case the Supreme Court ruled that a sit-down strike was not an illegal restraint of trade under the Sherman Anti-Trust Act when there was no intent to control trade.

Henry Ford decides to recognize the United Auto Workers union.

1938
The passage of the Merchant Marine Act creates a Federal Maritime Labor Board.

The Wages and Hours Act establishes a $.25 minimum wage, a 40-hour work week, and time and a half pay for hours worked beyond 40 a week. The act went into effect in October 1940 and was upheld in the Supreme Court on February 3, 1941.

The CIO became the Congress of Industrial Organizations with John L. Lewis as its president.

1936
The United Rubber Workers (CIO) staged the first large-scale sit-down strike and won recognition at Goodyear Tire and Rubber Company.

In Flint, Michigan, United Auto Workers made effective use of the sit-down strike at a General Motors plant, winning union recognition. Two months later company guards beat up UAW leaders at the River Rouge, Michigan plant.

The Anti-Strikebreaker Act (Byrnes Act) made it illegal to transport or aid strikebreakers in interstate or foreign trade.

The Public Contracts Act (Walsh-Healed Act) established labor standards, including minimum wages, overtime pay, child and convict labor provisions, and safety standards on all federal contracts.

1945 (con't)
The CIO affiliated with the newly created World Federation of Trade Unions. The AFL did not join because of the belief that the labor organizations of the Soviet Union were not "free and democratic."

President Franklin D. Roosevelt ordered the Army to seize the executive offices of Montgomery Ward after it violated a National War Labor Board directive regarding union shops.

1947
Congress passes the Taft-Hartley Act, restricting union activities and allowing states to pass "right-to-work" laws that prohibit closed union shops. President Harry Truman vetoed it, but Congress overrode the veto.

1948
Labor leader Walter Reuther is shot and seriously injured.

1950
President Truman orders the U.S. Army to seize all of the railroads to prevent a general strike. The railroads were kept under government control for two years.

1952
In April Truman orders the U.S. Army to seize the steel mills to avert a strike. In June the Supreme Court rules Truman's seizure illegal.

1956
A hit man blinds columnist Victor Riesel, who had fought against labor racketeers in New York City.

1957
AFL-CIO expels bakery workers, laundry workers and teamsters for corruption.

1955
The AFL merges with the CIO to form one of the largest labor organizations with membership estimated at 15 million.

In New Bedford and Fall River, Massachusetts, textile workers strike for a five cent raise. Union President Manuel "Manny" Fernandes Jr. leads the strike and successfully negotiates the nickel raise.

1949
An amendment to the Fair Labor Standards Act of 1938 is signed into law that directly prohibits child labor for the first time.

The CIO expels two unions at its annual convention on the grounds that they have communist leanings, and goes on to expel nine others by the mid 1950s during the Red Scare hysteria.

Unions from democratic countries withdrew from the World Federation of Trade Unions on the basis of its being dominated by communists. The International Confederation of Free Trade Unions was formed in London by labor representatives of 51 countries.

1946
The end of World War II ends wartime controls and unleashes frustrations that were pent up during the war, setting off the largest strike wave in history. Packing-house workers went on strike nationwide. More than 400,000 mine workers across the country went on strike. U.S. troops seized railroads and coal mines. The U.S. Navy seized oil refineries in order to break a strike that spread across 20 states.

Workers in packing houses go on strike across the country.

1959

Congress passes the Landrum-Griffen Act (Labor-Management Reporting and Disclosure Act) which regulated the internal affairs of unions in an attempt to rein in corruption.

The Supreme Court invokes the Taft-Hartley Act to break a steel strike.

1962

President John F. Kennedy signs an executive order to give federal employee's unions the right to bargain collectively with government agencies, opening the way for expansion of public sector bargaining rights in all levels of government.

1963

The longest newspaper strike in U.S. history ends, 100 days after the nine major newspapers in New York City had ceased publication.

Congress passes the Equal Pay Act prohibiting wage differences for workers based on sex.

1964

The Civil Rights Act is passed prohibiting discrimination in employment based on race, color, religion, sex or national origin.

1968

The Age Discrimination in Employment Act becomes law, making it illegal to discriminate in hiring or firing person between 40-65 on the basis of age.

The UAW leaves the AFL-CIO and joined the Teamsters in forming the Alliance for Labor Action (ALA).

Members of four railroad unions vote overwhelmingly to merge, creating the largest union merger in the railroad industry, known as the United Transportation Union (UTU).

1973

The major steel companies and the United Steelworkers of America approved an Experimental Negotiation Agreement through which the union gave up the right to strike in favor of binding arbitration. The companies agreed to end stockpiling of products.

Washington becomes the first state to allow the union shop for civil service employees.

1970

A walkout of postal carriers in Brooklyn and Manhattan begins the first mass postal strike in U.S. Postal Service history, eventually involving 210,000 of the nation's 750,000 postal employees. Mail Service was paralyzed in New York, Detroit, and Philadelphia. President Nixon declared a state of emergency and assigned military units to New York City post offices. The stand-off culminated two weeks later.

Hawaii became the first state to allow its state and local officials the right to strike.

Joseph A. Yablonski, a reform candidate who tried unsuccessfully to unseat "Tough Tony" Boyle as president of the United Mine Workers, is murdered, along with his wife and daughter, in their home in Clarksville, Pennsylvania by hit men acting on Boyle's orders. Boyle was later convicted of the killing. The next day West Virginia miners go on strike in protest.

Congress passes the Occupational Safety and Health Act (OSHA) mandating minimum standards of safety and healthy conditions in the workplace.

The United Farm Workers win an agreement with California grape growers after a five-year strike.

1974

The Coalition of Labor Union Women is formed in Chicago.

Congress passes the Employee Retirement Income Security Act, regulating the administration of pension funds.

The AFL-CIO created a public employee department in response to the growth of public employee unionism.

1977

Congress raises the minimum wage to $2.65.

1984

A strike against Hormel meat … fails to win its objectives. …

1986

More than 1,700 female flight attendants win $37 million in damages against United Airlines for firing them for getting married.

1989

Ninety eight miners and a minister occupy the Pittston Coal Company's Moss 3 preparation plant in Carbo, Virginia, setting off a year-long strike against Pittston Coal.

2011

Newly elected Wisconsin Republican Governor Scott Walker and the Republican-controlled state legislature, pass a law banning collective bargaining in relation to state jobs. Union demonstrations erupt in the state, recall campaigns are mounted, resulting in two Republican state senators being replaced by Democrats. A recall campaign was also launched against the governor. [results unknown at press time].

Ohio's newly elected Republican Governor John Kasich also pushed through a bill outlawing unions for government employees. The Ohio law went further than the Wisconsin law by including police and firefighters in its ban on collective bargaining. The law was defeated in a public referendum 61 to 39 percent.

1987

The 35-member executive council of the AFL-CIO decide unanimously to readmit the 1.6 million member Teamsters Union to its ranks, which had been expelled from the federation in 1957. President Jackie Presser was awaiting trial at the time, and the U.S. Justice Department was considering removal of the union's leadership because of possible links to organized crime.

1982

The Industrial Association of Machinists initiate a boycott against Brown & Sharpe, a tool manufacturer headquartered in Rhode Island, after the firm refused to bargain in good faith. The firm withdrew previously negotiated clauses in the contract and the union retaliated by initiating a strike during which the police sprayed pepper gas on 800 strikers at the company's North Kingston plant. A machinist narrowly escaped serious injury when a shot fired into the picket line hit his belt buckle. The National Labor Relations Board charged Brown & Sharpe with regressive bargaining, and entering into negotiations with the express purpose of not reaching an agreement with the union.

1981

Federal air traffic controllers launch a nationwide strike after their union rejects the government's final offer for a new contract. President Ronald Reagan fired most of the 13,000 striking controllers after they defied a back-to-work order and de-certified their union on the basis of an illegal strike.

1980

Joyce Miller becomes the first woman appointed to the AFL-CIO executive board.

1975

More than 80,000 members of the American Federation of State, County and Municipal Employees (AFSCME) mount the first legal large scale strike of public employees.

Chapter Three:

The Forgotten War—
The History of Class Struggle in America

History books that talk about America's wars list the Revolutionary War, the War of 1812, the Civil War, the Spanish American War, World Wars I and II, the Korean War, the Vietnam War, Iraq Wars I and II, and maybe a few more. But there is one major war that they don't list, the war between working people and big industrialist barons for human rights and fair treatment. Though it is not normally seen as a war, it was a war, and a long protracted one. It was an epic battle between large opposing forces that straddled the canvas of history. Many people were killed in the struggle for a five-day week, for an eight-hour day, for survivable working conditions, for wages a family could live on. Initially it was every man for himself against the giant corporations that owned the big industries: the railroads, coal, steel, oil, automobiles. It was one tiny person against a massive corporation representing accumulated capital and power of a group of people. Unions were the individual workers way of combining their power to defend themselves against the combined power of capital amassed by large corporations bent on profit and unconcerned with the well being or the rights of workers they needed to create their wealth. Only the shareholders were treated as people whose concerns mattered. Though workers were indispensable to the creation of profit, their wages were seen as expenses, which the corporation sought to hold to a minimum at all times in order to maximize profit and shareholder value.

The history of unions and the labor movement in America is the story of a vast social movement, made up of countless individual stories, struggles rising up independently in communities across the country. It is the story of the people who actually built America with their labors, as well as those who laid the foundations for equal rights and justice, extending the democratic franchise, building a strong middle class and making the American dream a reality for a growing portion of the population. The history of labor is diverse, made up of a broad and varied tapestry of events that could fill many volumes. In fact, Philip Foner wrote a 10-volume *History of the Labor Movement in the United States*, and even that does not tell the whole story.

The power struggle between labor and management has proceeded in a constant seesaw motion throughout the history of America. The history of that movement is characterized by one side gaining an advantage followed by the other side reasserting its advantage. Labor would make gains, then another of the many recurrent financial collapses would bring on an economic depression and labor would lose its gains. The cycle replayed itself over and over in many theaters of activity throughout American history.

Labor in Early America: Slaves and Indentured Servants

The American colonies that became the foundation of the United States were founded on largely free labor. In the cases of either slavery or indentured servitude the workers were almost totally at the mercy of their bosses. In the case of slaves, they were deemed animals with no rights and were totally under the control of those who claimed to own them. Just as in managing livestock, a slaveholder would have to provide enough in terms of food and lodging to keep his slaves alive and productive. Besides that virtually nothing limited the whims of the captor in terms of how he dealt with his slaves.

In the case of indentured servitude, the boss had almost total control over the servants and would often try to extend the period of servitude based on some claim against the servant alleging that the terms of the agreement were not kept.

Many of the early Americans were self employed, either on family farms or through their own trades and crafts. But it was never really a classless society. The class system of Europe was imported to the New World. Some colonists were given land grants by the British Crown, which supposedly owned the land in America and could partition it off to those who were in favor. A class of wealthy Americans was quickly established in the colonies, and they became the rulers of the new society. Those who orchestrated the American Revolution and became known as the Founding Fathers, were from the aristocratic, land-holding elite. Most of the unnamed soldiers who fought in the war were not.

Because of slavery and indentured servitude, the country developed a tradition of free labor, of servitude, of one class of controllers with power over another class of humans who had few if any rights. Slave labor drove the agricultural system that developed in the south and was so lucrative that it created an aristocratic class of cotton growers, a planter elite.

When evolving social forces challenged slavery, the southern planter elite held on fiercely to its free, captive labor and the aristocratic way of life that it financed. Since the planters had the capital and wielded the power, the whole south was dragged into the struggle to protect the slave system. It was only after President Lincoln proclaimed that the slaves were free that the war started to go in favor of the Union. When the energy of the slaves that had powered the southern economy was turned toward the hope of achieving freedom, the south collapsed.

Abraham Lincoln

In America slavery and forced labor are not relics from a deeply remote time in history. Slavery was a part of American life only a century and a half ago, until 1863 officially when Lincoln issued the Emancipation Proclamation. In the early 21st Century there are many living whose great- or great-great-grandparents lived in a world where slavery was part of the culture. The South did not just one day change its ways and abolish slavery, as many other countries did. The South only gave up slavery under gunpoint and after not only losing hundreds of thousands of its young men, but also suffering the devastation of total war on their lands as inflicted by northern armies rampaging through the south, waging war on civilian life as well as in the military battlefield.

The South, under the rule of the planter elite, held tenaciously to slavery and the belief in the entitlement of the aristocratic class to free labor to support their ease of life. The tradition of slavery has been vanquished from America for 150 years, but that is only several generations, not long enough for it to be eradicated from the social conditioning of those who experienced it, passed down from generation to generation. The sense of aristocratic privilege still exists, and some Americans retain the feeling that they should be entitled to free labor from others, whether at gunpoint, or through some other form of coercion.

Rebellions in Early America

Even though America really was a New World and a Land of Opportunity for those who emigrated from Europe, the class structure was imported to America. Some arrived with land grants, others as indentured servants, others as slaves. Those who had land grants from the crown, or were financially well off and well connected, had much different possibilities open to them than those who arrived carrying a seven-year indentured servant contract. Black Africans who arrived in shackles were not even given the rights or the recognition of being human.

But it really was a New World. At first all of its citizens except American Indians were immigrants, and they were a select group of people who had picked themselves up and managed to move their lives to a land far away, untamed and undeveloped. To have made the voyage, they must have shared some qualities of adventurousness, fortitude, will, aspiration and courage. They landed in a place that was wide open, cut loose from the old, established societies of Europe. When the aristocratic classes of the landed gentry tried to continue the behavior of the class culture of the Old World in America, they encountered a rowdy bunch.

The Anti-Renter Rebellion

As early as the 1600s there were rebellions against the Dutch patroonship culture, which had been transplanted into the Hudson Valley through the Dutch colony of New Amsterdam. Under the patroonship system, a few families aligned by intermarriage ruled over 300,000 people and 2 million acres of land. The largest landholder was the Rensselaer family, which ruled 80,000 tenants and had a fortune of approximately $41 million.

One of the periodic financial crises hit in 1837 and left many people unemployed. To make matters worse, there were many layoffs after the completion of the Erie Canal. In summer 1839 tenants of the Rensselaer estate gathered for a mass meeting and proclaimed, "We will take up the ball of the Revolution where our fathers stopped it and roll it to the final consummation of freedom and independence of the masses." Thousands of farmers joined together and formed an Anti-Renter association to stand together and prevent the landlords from evicting them. They put on Indian costumes in emulation of the Boston Tea Party, and 10,000 men were trained and ready. When a sheriff approached the area in fall of 1839 to collect back rents, he got a letter saying the group would no longer pay rent until they could be "redressed of their grievances" and that the tenants would now assume the right of doing to their landlord as he had to them, "as they please." And, the letter added, this was not "children's play," and "if you come out in your official capacity ... I would not pledge for your safe return."

A deputy brought writs demanding rent payments and the tenants seized the writs and burned them. He returned with a mounted posse of 500 and they were met by 1800 farmers blocking their path and 600 more blocking their rear, on horseback, armed with clubs and pitchforks, blowing tin horns. The sheriff's posse decided to turn back.

A petition for an anti-rent bill with 25,000 signers was put before the legislature, but the bill was defeated. The tensions continued for years in a simmering guerrilla war with thousands of farmers in revolt, and violence breaking out sporadically between sheriff's posses and bands of anti-renters in Indian clothing.

Under the leasing arrangement, landlords were legally allowed to help themselves to the timber on any of the farms under them. But during the tensions one of the men sent to get lumber was killed. When a deputy sheriff tried to collect $60 back rent by selling a farmer's livestock he was killed. The governor of New York declared a state of rebellion and sent 300 troops, who captured and imprisoned nearly a hundred Anti-Renters. Those who had been armed at the scene of the deputy's death were declared guilty of murder. Two were hanged and six were sentenced to life in prison. Two of the leaders escaped heavy sentences by agreeing to write letters urging other Anti-Renters to disband. The movement was finally crushed. The authorities convinced the rebels they could not win with physical force. They turned their energies to political organizing and managed to get 14 of their candidates elected to the state legislature.

In 1846, the new governor was elected with Anti-Renter support and he made good on a promise to pardon the convicted Anti-Renters. Court decisions in the 1850s placed some limits on the prerogatives of the landlords of the manorial system, but left the system in place. Tensions and sporadic uprisings continued for years. By 1869 Anti-Renters were still thwarting the efforts of sheriffs acting on behalf of the big landowners. In the 1880s only 2,000 of the 12,000 farmers who had been under lease in the 1840s were still under lease, but the system was still in place.

Thomas Dorr

Dorr's Rebellion

Around the same time as the Anti-Rent movement a rebellion broke out in Rhode Island that came to be known as Dorr's Rebellion. The anger of the rebels focused on the fact that Rhode Island's charter allowed only landholders to vote. As the population grew from people moving into the city from the farms and new immigrants coming from Europe, the number of disenfranchised grew, and with it the rancor and discontentment of the unrepresented masses. In 1833, Seth Luther, acting as a spokesman for working people, wrote the "Address on the Right of Free Suffrage," and denounced the monopoly of power held by "the mushroom lordlings, sprigs of nobility ... [and] small potato aristocrats." He advocated noncooperation with the government and refusal to pay taxes or serve in the militia. He posed the question: Why should 12,000 without the right to vote have to serve 5,000 who have land and can vote?

The rebellion gained momentum and came to be known as Dorr's Rebellion in honor of Thomas Dorr, a lawyer from an affluent family who became a leader of the suffrage movement, which advocated the expanding the right to vote. Working people formed the Rhode Island Suffrage Association and organized their own People's Convention, which produced an alternative state constitution that did not include land owning as a qualification for the right to vote. In 1842 they held their own vote and 14,000 people voted for the new constitution, including 5,000 who were landowners, a majority of the legal voters under the official charter. They also held an unofficial election in which Dorr was elected governor with 6,000 votes. Meanwhile the real governor of Rhode Island got President John Tyler to commit to sending troops in case of a rebellion.

The Dorr forces continued to go through the motions of establishing their own alternative state. On May 3, 1842, they held an inauguration with a parade of supporters marching through Providence. They convened their People's Legislature, and Dorr mounted an attack on the state's arsenal, which turned out to be a joke, with his cannon misfiring. The official governor ordered Dorr's arrest and he went into hiding.

Since the alternative charter had retained the qualification of "white" for voters, over Dorr's objections, the African Americans the area joined militia of the Law and Order coalition, which promised a new constitution that would give them the right to vote.

Dorr left the state to try to raise military support, but when he returned to Rhode Island, his hundreds of followers who were willing to fight for the People's Constitution were greatly outnumbered by thousands on the side of the state militia. The resistance collapsed and Dorr fled Rhode Island again. A hundred or so of the rebel militia were captured and imprisoned.

A new constitution extended the vote to those who would pay a $1 poll tax. When Dorr returned to the state in fall 1843, he was arrested and tried for treason. He was found guilty and sentenced to life in prison with hard labor. After Dorr had spent 20 months in prison, the new Law and Order party governor pardoned him.

The Dorr people took their case to the Supreme Court through a trespass suit against Law and Order militiamen. The case asserted that the alternative government was the real government of Rhode Island, but the Supreme Court ruled against it. The court accepted the argument of Daniel Webster, who argued the case against the Dorrites. If anyone can claim a constitutional right to overthrow an existing government, Webster had said, there would be chaos and anarchy.

The First American Unions

The earliest unions appeared in the 1790s, started by craft journeymen and shoemakers in Philadelphia, cabinet makers and printers in New York City, and tailors in Baltimore. In the early 1800s organizing spread into other professions, including carpenters, tailors and masons in New York, shoemakers in

Baltimore and Pittsburgh and printers in seven cities from Boston to New Orleans. They challenged the number of work hours and tried to get jobs for members and members only. But the new U.S. government had adopted laws based on English law that considered union organizing to be criminal conspiracy. So whenever some progress was made, organizers were charged with conspiracy and convicted.

The new government took power in 1789 and was controlled by the land-holding gentry, which split into two rival factions, the Federalists, dominated by wealthy financiers and merchants, and the Democratic Republicans, founded by Jefferson, which represented farmers, planters and artisans.

The election of Jefferson in 1800 initiated 24 years of Democratic-Republican rule. During that period the democratic franchise grew as the elitist Federalists lost their grip on power in state and local governments, which began to provide public education and expand the number of offices that were elected rather than appointed. In the mid 1820s the Federalists collapsed, and the rival factions of the Democratic Republicans split into the Whigs and the Democrats. By 1825 all but three states (Louisiana, Rhode Island and Virginia) granted voting rights to all white male citizens. All states except South Carolina and Delaware chose presidential electors by votes of the people, not state legislators. White servitude diminished.

In the south the planter elite ruled with an iron hand. In 1830 only a third of southern families owned slaves. By 1860 it was only a quarter. Though a minority, they used their power to run their states for the elite. There was a tremendous amount of money being made in the cotton industry, and the institution of slavery served the interests of the planters, and in the ancillary industries that served it, such as cotton brokers, shippers and slave traders. Northern capitalists also had a stake in the industries, especially the bankers who provided capital, the cotton traders and the textile factories.

The planter elite maintained its control through force. Armed posses policed country roads at night looking for signs of disturbance in the slave communities. Sentries patrolled the urban areas and state militias backed them up. Abolitionists were suppressed, intimidated or chased out. Workers were suppressed. Those who tried to organize were crushed by force backed up by court decisions.

In 1827 Philadelphia's craft unions formed the Mechanics' Union of Trade Associations. It was the first American labor organization that encompassed various trades. In 1828 its member unions formed the Working Men's Party, which ran candidates for public office. By the early 1830s similar parties appeared in more than 60 cities and towns. They advocated improved public education, an end to militia musters and a repeal of conspiracy laws against union organizing. The Democratic party adopted the positions, coopting the independent labor parties. But union members continued to organize for political action.

Between 1833 and 1836 craft unions established federations in 13 cities, coordinating efforts through the National Trades Union organized in 1834. They published newspapers, mobilized strikes, and advocated reforms, such as the reduction of the work day from 12 or more hours to 10. The NTU worked from the top down, petitioning the government to establish the 10-hour day while local unions organized strikes making the same demands.

In June 1835 the Philadelphia Trades Union organized the first general strike in U.S. history, with workers from 17 trades participating. After three weeks, the City Council gave municipal workers the 10-hour day with no reduction in pay. Private employers then did the same. The movement spread through craft unions across the mid Atlantic states and most were successful in winning the 10-hour work day.

The labor movement at the time went beyond the NTU action of the craft unions. Unskilled laborers and women also agitated for higher pay. Strikes were held by women tailors in New York and Baltimore, shoebinders in New York, Philadelphia and Lynn, Massachusetts, and textile workers in Lowell, Massachusetts. While working men were on general strike in Philadelphia in 1835, more than 500 working women formed a federation called the Female Improvement Society and struck for wage increases for the women who sewed uniforms for the U.S. Army. Irish canal workers held at least 14 strikes in the 1830s. New York dock workers, including coal heavers, stevedores and sailors held dozens of strikes in the 1830s.

Lowell Mill Women's Strikes (1834 and 1836)

In the early 1830s an economic boom had created many jobs at good wages but when economic activity leveled off, the owners of the Lowell mills cut wages 15 percent. The employees, mostly women, rebelled and stopped working. At the time the word "strike" was not even used, but the women improvised such a tactic out of anger. They were not successful in reversing the 15 percent pay cut and the women either returned to work at subsistence wages or left town. In 1936 the economy slowed even further. This time it was an increase in rent at the company boardinghouses that set off the spark of anger that led to mass action. The women formed a Factory Girls Association and instigated a strike that lasted several weeks, finally culminating with a return to previous rent levels. It was an early victory creating an example of how labor could exert power over employers.

Employers fought back by firing and blackballing union activists and taking unions to court. In 1835 New York's Supreme Court ruled against the shoemaker's unions that strikes and unions themselves were illegal under conspiracy law. In 1836 20 tailors were convicted of criminal conspiracy for strikes against companies that had reneged on wage agreements. Union members were fired and 27,000 people, about 20 percent of the population of the city, assembled in City Hall Park to protest the verdict.

With the law standing against the right to organize, the leaders of the NTU met to decide how the labor movement should proceed. Some advocated political organizing to try to repeal anti-union laws. Some advocated the establishment of worker-owned cooperative shops. But the financial panic of 1837 threw the country into a seven-year slump and layoffs were so widespread as to virtually destroy the NTU and nearly all unions.

At the same time labor had become a voting constituency worthy of courting, and Democrat and Whig politicians competed for the labor vote. President Martin Van Buren won labor support for Democrats by instituting the 10-hour day on federal construction projects in 1840. Competing with Democrats for the working class vote, the Whigs who wielded power on the Massachusetts Supreme Court passed a landmark ruling in the case of *Commonwealth versus Hunt* in 1842. In overturning a conspiracy charge against a bookmakers union in Boston the court declared that workers had the right to organize and to strike for "useful and honorable purposes." Under the new ruling, workers who shut down production, or tried to form a union, could no longer be charged with conspiracy.

But because of the economic depression, the two victories had little impact. The labor movement had been so weakened that there were few strikes and few conspiracy charges that the Massachusetts ruling could apply to. And unions could not force state governments to follow President Van Buren's lead with the 10-hour day.

Nevertheless, factory workers in the 1840s and 1850s continued to struggle for the 10-hour day. There was still no national labor organization to represent the laborers' interests, but in Massachusetts an association took root called the New England Workingmen's Association, which served as a galvanizing point around which the various local movements could align themselves. The workers saw the 10-hour day as a beginning of political reform of a broader nature. The idea caught on, spread by the labor press of the time. The organizations launched petition drives and campaigned for voters to demand legislation to limit the work day to 10 hours. Some state legislatures responded to the demands. New Hampshire passed a 10-hour workday law in 1847, followed by Maine and Pennsylvania in 1848, and in the 1850s New Jersey, Connecticut, Rhode Island, Ohio, Georgia and California. Finding ways around the laws for employers, however, was easy. The laws allowed "special contracts" to extend the workday beyond 10 hours, and many companies found it easy to force workers in desperate need of work to sign such contracts.

After the depression of 1839-1843, a new labor movement rose, but it was more fragmented and locally based than before the depression. National craft unions were created by workers in various trades, including printers, cigar makers, machinists and building trades workers. The first of this wave of national crafts unions was the National Typographical Union that was founded in 1852. In 1869 it changed its name to the International Typographical Union. It was a leader in the labor movement and still exists in the 21st Century.

From 1845 to 1856 a group calling itself the National Industrial Congress met every year and brought together a diverse collection of people including unionists, land reform advocates, cooperationists and others who would be considered radicals. In 1850, 46 organizations in New York City joined forces to create a group known as the Industrial Congress, which included not only trade unions, but National Reform Clubs, Christian labor reform groups, German socialist organizations, and cooperatives.

Chapter Four

The Civil War and Beyond

The Civil War was a second birth for the new country. In many ways the Civil War marks the end of the colonial period and the actual birth of a new nation. It was, however, a birth that was ridden with strife and bloodshed stemming from deep divisions within the society, some of which remain embedded in American society in the 21st Century.

The Civil War was the battleground upon which the high-flown aspirations for a free society expressed in the Declaration of Independence were put to the test. The old world colonial aristocracy was finally officially dethroned. It would never again be legal for one man to own another in America. It was a huge step toward fulfilling the promise of a society in which every man would be seen to have essential human rights.

But this is only one aspect of the Civil War. It was also an engine of industrialization that drove the growth of corporate power and wealth to heights never before seen. The war created a huge demand for a great many resources and manufactured goods. For some people war was very good business. It created opportunities for those who managed to find themselves a niche supplying the armed services or some other aspect of the great national war efforts. When the war drew to a close Lincoln would be able to put his attention on the corporate monster that had been given birth to by the war. But during the war, all considerations had to be put aside until the war was won and the United States was one nation intact.

In reaction to the increasing consolidation of power by large corporations, there was a growth of labor resistance to the oppressive and exploitative policies of the industrialists. The balance of power between labor and management seesawed back and forth over and over.

Labor organizing gathered force during the Civil War. Its initial focus was on achieving a shortening of the work day. By 1868 several states, including Wisconsin, Illinois, Missouri, Connecticut, Pennsylvania and New York, had passed laws limiting the work day to eight hours. The success of the efforts led the unions to increase their demands. More than a dozen new unions sprang up between 1868 and 1873. One was the National Labor Union, which proposed breaking down the large corporations and distributing the wealth more broadly. But the apparent initial success in legislating the eight-hour work day soon proved to be an illusion. The laws for the most part had no provisions for enforcement, and ultimately little effect. Many also included "free contract" provisions, which gave employers the right to come up with different arrangements if agreed to by workers. So in spite of the law, workers continued to work much more than eight hours a day.

Samuel Gompers, an early union activist who was highly influential in the history of labor, came to the conclusion that legislation was a pointless exercise and collective bargaining was the only way to bring any leverage to the issues with employers.

WORKING CLASS HEROES:
Samuel Gompers 1850-1924

In 1881, nine men met in Terre Haute, Indiana, to discuss the formation of a national order of workingmen. They set a conference in Pittsburgh in the fall and the attendees of the conference formed the Federated Trades and Labor Council, which later became

Samuel Gompers

the American Federation of Labor. It was led by Samuel Gompers, a 31-year old New York cigarmaker. He was a Jewish immigrant from the Jewish ghetto of London. He was short, not an impressive looking man, but he had an iron will and great passion for the cause of working people.

Gompers had learned from the bitter experience of broken strikes and had formulated a plan for a successful union. It was to organize all workers, control working conditions, and build the financial power of the union. Substantial dues were collected to finance unemployment and death benefits. The union found jobs for members. The union would not pay strike benefits unless it had called the strike. The policy acted as a deterrent against spontaneous strikes, or wildcat strikes, which were usually failures. The union lobbied for laws limiting the work day to eight hours, outlawing child labor and establish bureaus of labor statistics in all states.

Gompers was born in London January 27, 1850, to a poor Jewish family from Amsterdam. He attended London's Jewish Free School from ages 6 to 10 and then was pulled out of school by his parents and sent to work as an apprentice cigar maker. He continued his studies at night school, studying Hebrew and the Talmud. He later said those studies had some of the same benefits for the development of his mind as the study of law.

The Gompers family's economic situation was so desperate it left England to seek new opportunities in the New World, moving to New York in 1863. Gompers joined the cigar makers union at age 14. He helped his father manufacture cigars at home, but also participated in a debate club where he gained experience in constructing arguments, public speaking and parliamentary procedure. He also met other ambitious young men, including Peter J. McGuire, who would be an important ally and would play a role later with the AFL.

In 1873, at the age of 23, Gompers got a job with David Hirsch

& Company, one of the top cigar making shops. The factory was operated by a German immigrant who was a socialist. In that work environment Gomers came into contact with other German émigrés, who were, he wrote, "men of keener intellect and wider thought than any I had met before." He learned German and absorbed many ideas from his co-workers, including the ideas of socialism. He became particularly interested in the ideas of Karl Laurrell, the former secretary of the International Workingmen's Association. Laurrell became a mentor to him and persuaded him to get behind the trade union movement. Although he enjoyed the exchange of ideas at socialist meetings, he never joined the Socialist Party. Instead he followed Laurrell's advice and put his faith in unions.

Gompers was elected president of the Cigarmakers International Union Local 144 in 1875, but the union almost collapsed with the financial crisis of 1877, when jobs were few and labor was plentiful. Reductions in pay were happening almost on a daily basis and Gompers told workers they needed to organize to defend themselves. "The time has come when we must assert our rights as workingmen," he said. "Everyone present has the sad experience that we are powerless in an isolated condition, while the capitalists are united; therefore it is the duty of every cigar maker to join the organization. ... One of the main objects of the organization is the elevation of the lowest paid worker to the standard of the highest, and in time we may secure for every person in the trade an existence worthy of human beings."

In 1886 he was elected second vice president of the Cigarmakers International Union and in 1896 we was elected to first vice president, a position he held until his death in 1924. He helped to found the Federation of Organized Trades and Labor Unions in 1881. The organization was reorganized in 1886 as the American Federation of Labor. With the exception of the year 1895, he remained president until his death. Under his leadership, the AFL grew in influence, supplanting the Knights of Labor.

Gompers was a galvanizing leader who was able to help promote harmony among the various craft unions of the AFL. He believed the purpose of labor unions was to achieve the economic aspirations of their members, including higher wages, better working conditions, shorter hours so that they could enjoy what he called an American standard of living, in which they would be able to own their own homes, have ample food and decent clothing and the opportunity to provide their children an education. Union organizing and collective bargaining were the primary means to achieving those ends, he believed, but he also urged participation in the political system.

Gompers said the riot at Tompkins Square in 1873 convinced him of the futility of radicalism. Disgruntled people confronting authority in public places would not better the lot of the workingman, he concluded. Labor's rights could best be won through negotiation and the careful use of the workers' leverage over profits and production.

"What does labor want?" he said. "We want more school houses and less jails. More books and less guns. More learning and less vice. More leisure and less greed. More justice and less revenge. We want more ... opportunities to cultivate our better natures." Gompers' ideas formed the foundation of many union practices that continued throughout the 20th Century, including tactics of collective bargaining and the principles of contract negotiation.

Business Fights Back

In the cyclical fashion that characterizes labor history, after labor gains during the Civil War period, a backlash developed and business owners unleashed a new wave of repression against union organizers using security agencies, local police forces and state militias. Meanwhile in Paris in 1871 thousands of workers and soldiers took control of the city, elected their own government, reopened closed factories as cooperatives, burned the guillotine and declared separation of church and state. After two months, the French Army regained control of Paris and 30,000 workers were killed. American workers identified with the movement in France. Many held meetings and raised money to send in support of the revolutionaries. The Paris Commune, as it came to be called, was the first event to be communicated across the new transatlantic cable, and the news instilled fear in American elites. They took steps to prepare themselves to counter any similar uprisings from American workers. After the Paris Commune incident, anti-labor repression greatly intensified. Organizers became identified as "communists," the dreaded enemy of society.

The Panic of 1873

After the Civil War, soldiers returned home and flooded labor markets. Former slaves also entered the job market. A financial collapse in Europe in the 1870s bled over into the U.S., and brought down the top investment banking firm in the country, Jay Cooke. The Cooke firm was the main financial backer of the Northern Pacific Railroad and was a major investor in other railroads. It also acted as a conduit for the government's war loans. When it collapsed it sent a huge ripple through the economic system. The New York Stock Exchange was closed for 10 days, foreclosures and factory closings became common occurrences, 89 of the country's 364 railroads went bankrupt and 18,000 businesses failed in the period between 1873 and 1875. By 1876, unemployment rose to 14 percent. Those who still had railroad jobs only had work for half of the year, and their salaries were cut 45 percent to a dollar a day. The crash became known as the Panic of 1873.

The Panic of 1873 set off several years of economic depression. It was known as the Great Depression until the 1930s when the name was borrowed to refer to that depression and historians renamed the depression of the 1870s "The Long Depression."

After the collapse of 1873, the rapid economic expansion of the U.S. that had been fueled primarily by the growth of the railroads stopped dead. The Baltimore & Ohio cut wages, then cut them a second time within the year. The second cut set off a firestorm of reaction. A strike erupted in several states, focused primarily in the major cities of Pennsylvania, Maryland, Illinois, and Missouri. Rail traffic in major cities like Pittsburgh came to a halt. The U.S. Supreme Court declared strikes illegal. Unemployed people took to wandering the country, gathering in camps, demonstrating for relief. In New York, St. Louis, and Chicago camps were attacked by mounted police. Some legislators advocated feeding poisoned food to tramps.

The Destruction of the Molly Maguires

By 1877 a fifth of the nation's work force was unemployed. In the anthracite coal mines in Eastern Pennsylvania in the late 1870s, the wars between industrialists and labor became particularly brutal. Incidents of violence became common, many people were killed. Tensions developed to the point of open warfare. A group of Irish American miners who had been members of a secret society in Ireland known as the Molly Maguires were known to be violent and were targeted by the major industrialists for "extermination." In part because the Molly Maguires was a secret society, the facts of its story are blurry and still controversial.

In the 1870s there were 22,000 miners working in coal mines in Schuylkill County, Pennsylvania, in extremely difficult conditions. That number included 5,500 children between the ages of seven and 17 who earned between a dollar and three dollars a week to separate slate from coal. Wages were low and working conditions were dreary and deadly. Miners crawled in narrow crevices over mud and through dripping water lighting the way with lamps and constantly breathing coal dust, which eventually led to lung disease. Deaths from accidents, fires or collapses were frequent. Hundreds of miners were killed in accidents every year. In 1869 a fire broke out at the Avondale Mine in Luzerne County, and since the coal company had repeatedly refused requests to provide emergency exits, as many as 179 miners were burned to death.

John Siney

As the bodies were brought out of the mine, John Siney, the head of the Workingmen's Benevolent Association spoke to thousands of miners gathered there. "If you must die with your boots on, die for your families, your homes, your country, but do not longer consent to die like rats in a trap for those who have no more interest in you than in the pick you dig with." A thousand miners signed up for the union that day.

Frank B. Gowen

Frank B. Gowen, who was president of both the Philadelphia and Reading Railroad and of the Philadelphia and Reading Coal and Iron

Company, hired the Pinkerton Detective Agency to infiltrate the Mollies. Allan Pinkerton assigned agent James McParlan to collect evidence against the Mollies of their involvement in any of the unsolved murders or plots of rebellion. Gowen organized mine owners into an organization called the Anthracite Board of Trade. When the union grew to a membership of 30,000, 85 percent of the miners in Pennsylvania, Gowen decided to force a showdown with the union.

James McParlan

Some of the members of the union were allegedly members of the Mollies. The Ancient Order of Hibernians was an organization that some historians think was a cover for the Mollies. The coal miners union, the Workingmen's Benevolent Association, was peaceful, and the AOH was also seen as a peaceful fraternal order. But the Pinkertons believed they found a connection between the AOH's membership and violent areas in Ireland. McParlan thought the Mollies had merely taken on a new name with the AOH. But while the Mollies were seen to be violent, the union used peaceful methods and had in its five-year existence improved the relations between labor and management. The Pennsylvania Bureau of Industrial Statistics determined that the union had brought an end to violence that had been ongoing since the Civil War. The union's leaders were opposed to the Molly Maguires.

By the time of the Panic of 1873, Gowen was convinced he wanted to break the power of the union and weed out and exterminate its Molly Maguire members. In December 1874 Gowen led a move among the coal mine operators to cut pay by 20 percent. The miners responded by going on strike on January 1, 1875. War erupted between miners and owners. In March Edward Coyle, a union leader who was a member of AOH, was murdered. Another member of AOH was shot dead by a mine superintendant. A mine boss fired into a group of miners. A band of vigilantes attacked a union meeting and killed one miner and wounded several others. Allan Pinkerton decided to hire vigilantes to make examples of the Mollies. In December 1875 masked men attacked three men and two women who had been identified as Mollies in their home. At least one of the men and a woman, the wife of one of the men, were shot and killed. When McParlan heard that vigilantes had been given the information he had uncovered and used it not only to kill suspected members of the Mollies, but also a woman he considered an innocent bystander, he resigned. "I am not going to be an accessory to the murder of women and children."

The leader of the vigilantes was arrested, then released on bail. Another miner who had been identified by McParlan as a killer was shot and wounded and later his house was attacked by gunmen. The war continued with more killings and revenge killings on both sides. A man was found with his throat cut, another crucified in the woods, a mining boss mauled, a telegraph office burned, a train derailed.

The union leaders were imprisoned, vigilantes conducted attacks on the strikers, many of the Mollies were killed and the strike was broken. Starving miners went back to work, accepting the pay cut.

When murder trials of the alleged Mollies began, Gowen was appointed special prosecutor. Irish Catholics were not allowed to be on the jury. But Welshmen, who had been the enemies of the Irish, were well represented. Most of the prosecution witnesses were employees of the railroad and mining companies that were trying to destroy the union. Most of the victims of the unsolved murders had been employees of the small railroad companies that had been taken over by the Philadelphia and Reading Railroad Company. The private corporation initiated the investigation through a private detective agency. A private police force arrested the accused and private attorneys prosecuted them. Twenty men were convicted of various murders and hanged.

In 1883, Gowen retired as president of the company. In 1889 he locked himself into a hotel room and shot himself in the head. In 1979 Pennsylvania Milton Shapp granted a posthumous pardon to Jack Kehoe on the recommendation of the Pennsylvania Board of Pardons and proclaimed that the "men called Molly Maguires" were heroes in the struggle to form a union.

Mother Jones

WORKING CLASS HEROES:
Mother Jones 1837-1930

The person who became known as Mother Jones was born Maria Harris in Cork, Ireland. Her family emigrated to Canada when she was 14 or 15 years old. She attended Toronto Normal School and trained to be a teacher. Her family moved to the U.S. and she took a job teaching in Monroe, Michigan. Then she moved to

Chicago and worked as a dressmaker, and in 1861 she moved to Memphis, Tennessee, and married George Jones, an iron molder and union organizer. She opened a dress shop in Memphis. Then she lost her entire family to a disease.

"In 1867, a yellow fever epidemic swept Memphis," she wrote in her autobiography. "Its victims were mainly among the poor and the workers. The rich and the well-to-do fled the city. Schools and churches were closed. People were not permitted to enter the house of a yellow fever victim without permits. The poor could not afford nurses. Across the street from me, ten persons lay dead from the plague. The dead surrounded us. They were buried at night quickly and without ceremony. All about my house I could hear weeping and the cries of delirium. One by one my four little children sickened and died. I washed their little bodies and got them ready for burial. My husband caught the fever and died. I sat alone through nights of grief. No one came to me. No one could. Other homes were as stricken as mine. All day long, all night long, I heard the grating of the wheels of the death cart."

After her family was gone she got a permit to help nurse the sick and did so until the end of the plague. Then she moved back to Chicago and opened her own sewing business, working for some of the wealthiest families in Chicago. "I had ample opportunity to observe the luxury and extravagance of their lives," she wrote. "Often while sewing for the lords and barons who lived in the magnificent houses on the Lake Shore Drive, I would look out of the plate glass windows and see the poor, shivering wretches, jobless and hungry, walking along the frozen lake front. The contrast of their condition with that of the tropical comfort of the people for whom I sewed was painful to me. My employers seemed neither to notice or to care."

Her seamstress business was destroyed in The Great Chicago Fire in 1871, which destroyed everything she had and left thousands of people homeless. The loss of her business on top of the loss of her family caused her to go through a deep questioning process

over her destiny and what she was to do with the rest of her life. She began attending meetings of the Knights of Labor, listening to the speakers with great interest. She learned of the formation of the Knights of Labor when at the close of the Civil War men who had recently been fighting as "blues" or "grays" over the issue of chattel slavery joined together to fight another form of slavery—industrial slavery. Mother Jones joined the Knights and immersed herself in the cause of labor. By 1880, she had devoted herself completely to the welfare of working people. After the Knights of Labor faded in influence in the 1890s, Mother Jones worked primarily with the United Mine Workers.
"Those were the days of sacrifice for the cause of labor," she wrote. "Those were the days when we had no halls, when there were no high salaried officers, no feasting with the enemies of labor. Those were the days of the martyrs and the saints."

Jones participated in many of the actions at the time. It was a time of widespread turmoil as industrial America got its footing and began to grow up in the ruins of the Civil War. She participated in the Great Railroad Strike of 1877, was present at the Haymarket Incident and countless other important events of the labor movement.

"These early years saw the beginning of America's industrial life," she wrote. "Hand in hand with the growth of factories and the expansion of railroads, with the accumulation of capital and the rise of banks came anti-labor legislation, came strikes, came violence, came the belief in the hearts and minds of workers that legislatures but carry out the will of the industrialists."

She was bold and gutsy and seemed to fear nothing. She faced down guns, fists and clubs, and with her courage she shamed her adversaries into impotence. She became a well-known figure, loved by the workers and loathed by the coal mining and railroad companies. Her presence could lift the morale of large numbers of people and catalyze a turning point in a struggle.

She improvised unique methods: during the miner strikes she

organized miners' wives armed with mops and brooms to guard the mines against scabs. She became known as "The most dangerous woman in America" after a West Virginia district attorney gave her that title. She was crafty and resourceful, able to find an unexpected tactic at a difficult moment to turn a situation around.

When she was called in to help at a coal miners' strike in Clarksburg, West Virginia, she camped in open fields and held meetings in barns, preaching the gospel of unionism. The Consolidated Coal Company that owned the company town of New England would not allow the distribution of notices of the union meeting and would arrest anyone caught with a notice. "But we got the news around," wrote Jones. "Several of our men went into the camp. They went in twos. One pretended he was deaf and the other kept hollering in his hear as they walked around, 'Mother Jones is going to have a meeting Sunday afternoon outside of town on the sawdust pile.'"

The meeting attracted a large turnout, and when it was over Mother Jones proceeded to Fairmont City. When she and a young miner's lad approached the Company Store it was guarded by gunmen. One of them asked, "Who are you?"

"Mother Jones and a miner's lad," she answered.

"So that's you," said the gunman. "Mother Jones," rattling his gun.

"Yes, it's me," said Jones, "and be sure you take care of the store tonight. Tomorrow I'll have to be hunting a new job for you." She sent the young boy home, and got out of her buggy to wait for the three miners who were supposed to meet her there. Then she heard cries of "Murder! Murder!" and one of the miners came running up, crying, "They're killing Jo—on the bridge—the gunmen!"

"At that moment the Interurban car drove up," Jones wrote. "It would stop at the bridge. I thought of a scheme. I ran onto the bridge, shouting, 'Jo! Jo! The boys are coming. They're coming! The whole bunch is coming. The car is almost here.' Those bloodhounds for the coal company thought an army of miners was in the Interurban car. They ran for cover, barricading themselves in the company store. "They left Jo on the bridge, his head broken and the blood pouring from him," she wrote. "I tore my petticoat into strips, bandaged his head, helped the boys to get him on to the Interurban car, and hurried the car into Fairmont City. We took him to the hotel and sent for a doctor who sewed up the great, open cuts in his head. I sat up all night and nursed the poor fellow. He was out of his head and thought I was his mother."

In 1903, Mother Jones organized a Children's March from Philadelphia to President Theodore Roosevelt's home in Oyster Bay, New York, to protest the lax enforcement of child labor laws. She organized children who were working in the mines and mills and they marched, carrying banners saying, "We want to go to school and not the mines!" She had not been able to get the newspapers to write about the children with their missing fingers and other disabilities from their labors because the mill owners held stock in all the newspapers. So she devised the march as a way to get publicity in spite of the media blackout.

In 1905 she was one of the co-founders of the Industrial Workers of The World in Chicago, which attempted to organize all workers together, not keeping them separate as did the AFL. Mother Jones died in 1930 and is buried in the Union Miners Cemetery in Mount Olive, Illinois.

The Haymarket Incident

In the 1880s labor went through another cycle of rise and fall. In 1881 the Knights of Labor, which had been a secret union since its formation in 1869, went public with a Declaration of Principles that challenged corporate power. "The alarming development and aggressiveness of great capitalists and corporations, unless checked, will inevitably lead to the pauperization and hopeless

degradation of the toiling masses. It is imperative, if we desire to enjoy the full blessings of life, that a check be placed on the unjust accumulation, and the power of evil of aggregated wealth." The association grew from 43,000 members in 1882 to 730,000 in 1886. The group was organized into 15,000 locals around the country. In 1886, members of the Knights struck against Jay Gould's railroads in the Southwest, and Gould responded with deadly force. In East St. Louis, seven workers were killed by company deputies.

On May 1, 1886, the Knights of Labor sponsored a nationwide strike for the eight-hour day. Three hundred fifty thousand workers walked off jobs in 11,000 workplaces. Chicago police fired into a crowd of demonstrators, killing four. At Haymarket Square a crowd gathered to protest the shootings and it led to a tragedy that became known as the Haymarket Riot or the Haymarket Massacre. But it began as an orderly protest until an unknown person dropped a bomb out of a window. The bomb killed a number of people, including seven police officers. The incident set in motion a wave of hysteria as the public responded angrily to the killing of the policemen and the newspapers kept the story burning hot while the hysteria rose.

Mother Jones describes the incident in her autobiography. After many strikes in the 1880s, workers in Chicago were agitating for an eight-hour day. The trade unions and the Knights of Labor endorsed the movement. Because many of the leaders of the movement were immigrants who had left Europe to escape oppression, the establishment said the movement was foreign or used the cry of anarchism to discredit the movement. Some of the "foreign agitators" preached ideas of radical reorganization of society, such as socialism or anarchism, but the workers just wanted to shorten the work day to eight hours and to be paid a wage they could feed their families on.

It was a cold winter and the soup kitchens could not handle the number of applicants. People went hungry. On Christmas day, hundreds of poverty stricken people clad in rags marched in front of the mansions of the rich on Prairie Avenue. They carried the black flag of anarchism. The presence of the flag aroused fear and anger. The newspapers helped stoke the fear until May 1 when an uprising for the eight-hour day was scheduled. Employers feared revolution.

Workers from the McCormick Harvester Works assembled in front of the factory and tensions grew. Those who didn't join the strike were called scabs. Bricks were thrown, windows were broken, so-called scabs were threatened. The police swooped down on the strikers, shooting, clubbing, and trampling workers under horses. A number of them were shot dead and others, including young girls, were clubbed to death.

The Pinkerton Detective Agency formed armed bands of hoodlums and ex-convicts and hired them out to the capitalists to picket factories and stir up trouble. On May 4th the anarchists held a meeting in a district that became known as Haymarket Square only a half block from the police station. The mayor attended the gathering, found it to be orderly, and instructed the police chief not to send the police. But the chief of police went ahead and sent a large contingent of mounted police to the scene. As one of the anarchists addressed the crowd someone dropped a bomb from a window. It killed several police.

"The city went insane and the newspapers did everything to keep it like a madhouse," wrote Mother Jones. "The workers' cry for justice was drowned in the shriek for revenge. Bombs were 'found' every five minutes. Men went armed and gun stores kept open nights. Hundreds were arrested." But in the end, only those who had agitated for the eight-hour week were tried and a few months later hanged.

The Pullman Strike of 1894

Another cycle of labor expansion followed by repression took place in the 1890s. The establishment took to using court injunctions as a weapon in the war against labor. In 1894, Eugene V. Debs organized a sympathy strike in support of workers striking against the Pullman Palace Car Company and the company's lawyer met with U.S. Attorney and succeeded in getting a court injunction against the strike and ordering Debs to stop it. The case used the Sherman Antitrust Act, which had originally been drafted to limit corporate abuses of power, to win the injunction. Pullman argued that the strike disrupted postal service and interstate commerce and damaged the general welfare. With an injunction, there was no need to consult a jury, which might sympathize with workers, and made it possible to imprison union leaders for contempt of court if the strike took place. From 1880 to 1930 more than 4,000 injunctions were declared against strikes.

George Pullman

Great Railroad Strike of 1877

At the end of the Civil War, a huge wave in railroad construction began. Between 1866 and 1873 35,000 miles of track were laid coast to coast. Railroads became the second largest employer after farming. They required huge capital investment and entailed a proportionate amount of risk. It became a good field for speculators, which stimulated overexpansion. Jay Cooke was investing a large proportion of investor's funds in railroads, helping to set the stage for the collapse.

When the collapse of 1873 came, the economic pressure strained employer-employee relationships between railroad corporations and workers. Working conditions became increasingly harsh and predatory. Wages were cut. Workdays were extended. Strikes among the railroad workers began to break out, a number of which brought the trains to a halt. Most of the strikes were crushed by the railroads.

The Brotherhood of Locomotive Firemen, the professional association that represented railroad workers, saw itself primarily in an insurance function and didn't recognize strikes as a way to negotiate with employers. Since the BLF was not meeting enough of the needs of the workmen, membership declined. The workers wanted a union that would stop the train wrecks, raise pay, shorten hours and get the boss off the workers' backs. The BLF faded in influence and by the time the workers did mount a major strike against the railroad in 1877, the BLF had little to do with it. When both the Pennsylvania and Baltimore & Ohio railroads posted notices of pay cuts, the second round in a year, the workers revolted in an explosion of rage. The workers declared that they would not let the trains roll unless the second pay cut was revoked.

In Pennsylvania, Maryland and West Virginia groups of strikers blocked tracks to keep "scabs" (non-union people who went to work for a company when union workers were on strike) from operating the railroad. The revolt spread to Pittsburgh where a mob burned several stores. Pinkerton agents and state militia began to move against the strikers and President Rutherford B. Hayes sent troops into West Virginia and Maryland at the request of state governments. But the local militia refused to fire on the strikers. Soldiers brought in from Philadelphia, however, did not refuse the order and they killed 26 unarmed people.

Members of other unions, the Locomotive Engineers and the Order of Railway Conductors, went to work for the railroads as strike breakers. The railroads, state militia, Pinkertons, federal troops and other unions were aligned against the strikers, and they prevailed. They replaced the strikers with new hires. More than a hundred strikers were killed. Several hundred were wounded.

The strike spread to Chicago and St. Louis, creating more violence and death. Hayes sent troops into city after city to put down the strikes and riots, and finally, 45 days after it had begun, it ended. The strike was broken and the strikers were begging for their jobs back. But strikers were blacklisted and unable to work there anymore.

Eugene V. Debs

Working Class Heroes

Eugene V. Debs (1855-1926)

Eugene V. Debs was born five years before the outbreak of the Civil War to French immigrants in Terre Haut, Indiana. His father was well educated and sophisticated, but struggled hard to gain a foothold in the New World. Eugene was too young when the war was going on to understand the issues at stake, but years later studying history, he saw a hero in John Brown. "History may be searched in vain for an example of noble heroism and sublime self-sacrifice equal to that of Old John Brown," he wrote. "From the beginning of his career to its close he had but one idea and one ideal, and that was to destroy Chattel slavery; and in that cause he sealed his devotion with his noble blood. Realizing that his work was done, he passed serenely, almost with joy, from the scenes of men. His calmness upon the gallows was awe-inspiring; his exaltation supreme."

Sitting under busts of Voltaire and Rousseau, he listened to his father read from Racine, Corneille, Goethe and Schiller. His favorite work was Victor Hugo's *Les Miserables,* which he returned to periodically throughout his life. He learned to speak French and German and learned about the democratic traditions of Europe. He worked long hours in his parents' store growing up, and dreamed of going to work for the railroad. In 1870 he quit high school to go to work to help support the family, and to pursue his dream of working on the railroad. He found a job cleaning grease from railroad engines. But once on the job his romanticism of the railroads collided with the grim reality of working long hours daily in a cold, damp shop, with the potash he used to clean the grease eating into his skin until his hands were raw and his knuckles bloody. He worked for 50 cents a day and was low man on the totem pole. He had to take abuse from everyone over him, who were taking out their frustrations over being abused by those over them.

One night when a fireman didn't show up for work, Debs was put on the job. He became a fireman, keeping the coal burning in the engines, with hot flames on one side and snow blowing through the open cab. It was hazardous work and at times he regretted his decision to quit school. He tried to further his studies, but work took most of his time and energy. Then the Northern Pacific Railroad collapsed in a scandal of fraud and bribery in which congressmen participated. There were no more railroad jobs in Terre Haute. Debs rode the freights to Evansville, Indiana, to find work, and unable to find work there moved on to St. Louis, Missouri.

It was the largest city he had ever seen. In the wake of the current depression, many had lost their jobs. Families were pushed from their homes and many homeless people wandered the streets aimlessly. Makeshift shanties sprung up along the Mississippi River. Children rolled around in the mud and even ate it. It was the worst conditions for human beings he had seen in his life, as bad as what he had read about in his favorite book *Les Miserables*. The experience solidified his identification with and compassion for working people, which would guide him throughout his life.

He found work in St. Louis as a railroad fireman, and continued trying to educate himself, reading everything he could get hold of on a wide range of subjects. He became an authority on railroading. In 1874, at the insistence of his mother, he finally turned his back on working on the railroad. The railroads were becoming increasingly hazardous for workers because the companies were cutting costs by letting equipment wear out. Tracks were not well maintained and frequently broke. Defective boilers exploded, starting fires in the cars. Bridges collapsed. Injuries and deaths were common, and little attention was paid unless those who died were passengers. He was still only 19 years old when he quit. But the experience had molded some of the attitudes he would carry with him throughout his life.

Debs returned to Terre Haute and took a job as a billing clerk. But he didn't like the work and he didn't like business very much. One evening when he was in a saloon he heard that Joshua Leach, the Grand Master of the Brotherhood of Locomotive Firemen, was coming to Terre Haute to organize a union. Though he knew nothing of unions and was not working for the railroad anymore, he went to the meeting and was very inspired by Leach's vision of firemen joining together for a common cause. It reminded him of the spirit of the French Revolution: Liberty, Equality, Fraternity!

Debs was initiated into the Vigo Lodge and it ushered in a new way of life for him. It brought together his romantic feelings about railroads, with the ideals he learned at the knee of his father.

Debs and The Strike of 1877

The railroads consolidated in the 1850s and became increasingly harsh and predatory. Wages were cut. Workdays were extended. Strikes among the railroad workers began to break out, but most were crushed by the railroads.

Debs worked hard and rose quickly to leadership status in the union. But the BLF was not meeting the needs of the workmen and membership was declining. The workers wanted a union that would stop the wrecks, raise pay, shorten hours and get the boss off the workers' backs. The union faded in influence and by the time the workers did mount a strike against the railroad in 1877, the union had little to do with it. The Pennsylvania and Baltimore & Ohio railroads had posted notices of pay cuts and the workers revolted. (see below)

The failure of the Railroad Strike of 1877 had a profound effect on Debs. By then he was a national officer in the BLF. He blamed the railroads' oppression for forcing the strike to happen, but was even more concerned with the violence and lawlessness that took place during the strike. In a speech to BLF's national convention soon after the incident, he proclaimed that the union did not encourage such behavior.

The depression of 1873 put farmers in the squeeze between falling prices for their goods and increasing costs in mortgage rates, farm equipment and price gouging by the railroad. The unions had been effectively squashed by the railroads and working people were looking to the political system for some relief. Debs was swept into the fervor of the moment. He distinguished himself as a powerful public speaker for the causes of the poor and oppressed and the Democratic party. Local Democratic leaders noticed his talent and offered him the Democratic nomination for Congress. He declined because he didn't want to leave his family. But the next year he was elected city clerk of Terre Haute. Terre Haute's West End was a center of ginmills and prostitution. One of Debs' duties was to go after the fines owed by prostitutes who had been picked up. But Debs couldn't bring himself to come down hard on the struggling working women when the cops had been ineffective in bringing the pimps and racketeers to justice.

While city clerk, he kept his association with the BLF and soon found himself challenged to save the organization from collapse, which seemed eminent. The strike of 1877 had all but destroyed the BLF. While the officers were trying to think of ways to save the union, the railroads were looking for ways to destroy it once and for all. But Debs' courage and resolve never faltered.

One day a BLF officer was thrown out of the office of the vice president of the Pennsylvania Railroad. When Debs heard about it, he took the officer with him from Terre Haute back to the president's office in Columbus. When they walked into the office the vice president said, "Before we go any further I want you to know, Debs, that I don't give a God damn for the Brotherhood of Locomotive Firemen." Debs came back, "And I want you to know that I don't give a God damn for the Pennsylvania Railroad. I'm not here to get your opinion. I'm here to get courteous treatment for our officials." The two argued furiously for an hour and then the railroad executive offered Debs a job with the railroad. Debs refused. He also refused the offer of a free pass on the Pennsylvania Railroad, but he accepted a ticket back to Terre Haute. There was no more trouble with the railroad for the next few months and the word spread about how Deb had stood up to the VP of the railroad. His reputation grew and drew members into the union. He had shown by example that labor disputes could be solved by reason and compromise.

When his second terms as city clerk of Terre Haute was done, Debs went on the road helping to set up lodges for BLF across the country. He became known as a labor leader. Men came to him with problems. He investigated every railroad accident and used his findings when proposing legislation for safety.

He held on to his belief that labor disputes could be settled with reason, without resorting to strikes. He ignored the more radical

Gompers ideas and said that BLF was an insurance organization, not a trade union. He tried to develop friendly relations with the railroads. But the railroads were hostile.

Still seeking legislative remedies to labor problems and not strikes, Debs ran for congress and was elected, taking office in January 1885. He drafted a bill to force railroads to compensate workers for injuries while on duty. It passed the House of Representatives, but was eviscerated in the Senate, so that Debs felt he had failed the railroad workers. He was frustrated in most of his attempts to accomplish anything in Congress, so when his term was up, he didn't go for a second one.

Some of the railroads tried to undermine the Brotherhood by setting up compulsory insurance plans that would take away the main reason to join. It forced Debs to alter his position about strikes. He added new features to Brotherhood membership, including written contracts with employers, negotiated through strikes if necessary. The changes were in part a reaction to the success of the AFL, which was gaining members and affirming the popularity of the ideas of Gompers.

Debs was deeply embittered by the Homestead Strike (see below), which became a brutal war. In the BLF's *The Magazine,* he wrote, "If the year 1892 taught the workingman any lesson worthy of heed, it was that the capitalist class, like a devilfish, had grasped them; with its tentacles and was dragging them down to fathomless depths of degradation. To escape the prehensile clutch of these monsters constitutes a standing challenge to organized labor for 1893 and demands of workingmen an amount of sentinel duty which must be performed if victory is to perch upon their banners."

Efforts were made to create alliances among the labor organizations. The Knights of Labor, by then in decline and a shadow of itself in its heyday, met with the AFL in Philadelphia and again in St. Louis to figure out how to join forces. But they were unable to come to terms. Among the railroad unions the desire to join together was strong.

Debs was one of the founders of the American Railway Union (ARU), which was the first industrial union in America. When the union led a strike against the Pullman Car Company in 1894, President Grover Cleveland sent the army to break the strike. As one of the leaders of the union, Debs was imprisoned for refusing to obey an injunction, though he had initially tried to persuade members against going on strike before finally going along with it. While he was in prison he studied socialism. When he got out of prison, he launched a political career, running for president as a socialist in 1900, 1904, 1908, 1912 and 1920. The last time he ran for president was from a prison cell.

In 1905 he was one of the founders of the Industrial Workers of the World (IWW) in Chicago, a group of socialists, anarchists and radical trade unionists from across the country. Other founders included William D. ("Big Bill") Haywood, Daniel De Leon, Thomas J Hagerty, Lucy Parsons, "Mother" Mary Harris Jones, Frank Bohn, William Trautmann, Vincent Saint John and Ralph Chaplin. The goal was to promote worker solidarity and to overthrow the rule of the employer class. It was organized in part as a reaction to the AFL, which the IWW's founders (known as Wobblies) saw as having failed to effectively organize workers by keeping different categories separate. The Wobblies wanted to unite all workers as a class. It was conceived as an industrial union as opposed to a craft union, as was the AFL. IWW was the first organization to welcome all workers, including women, immigrants, African Americans and Asians.

In 1918 Debs gave a speech opposing U.S. involvement in World War I and was arrested, charged and convicted under the Espionage Act of 1917. He was sentenced to 10 years in prison. In 1921 President Warren G. Harding commuted his sentence. He died in 1926.

The Homestead Strike

By 1892, a small group of corporations that had grown extremely powerful since the Civil War, was wielding tremendous political clout in Washington and virtually controlling many state governments. All major appointments were given to members of the business elite. Legislation was a commodity for sale to the highest bidder. Industrialism had produced a handful of enormous fortunes made through silver, oil, transportation, timber and manufacturing. The capacity of industry to create mass profits created a new class of aristocracy in the U.S., which came to be known as the Robber Barons. They were almost incomprehensibly wealthy and used their wealth to wield political power. It had created an insurmountable advantage in the case of the strike of 1877 when workers found themselves pitted against a coalition that included railroads, state militia, Pinkertons, federal troops and other hostile unions. The biggest threat to the financial elites was unions, and they were ready to take stern measures in dealing with workers who weren't happy with their pay or working conditions. In the early 1890s the country was in another depression and conflicts between labor and management kicked up all over the country. In 1890 the price for rolled-steel products started to decline, from $35 a gross ton to $22 in 1892. Henry C. Frick, the general manager of the Carnegie Steel plant in Homestead, Pennsylvania, wanted to cut wages and while he was at it, he wanted to break the workers' union, The Amalgamated Association of Iron and Steel Workers, which was one of the strongest unions in the country. The company had persuaded Congress to raise the tariff on steel billets so it could afford to pay higher wages, but then instead demanded a pay cut. As the deadline for contract negotiations approached, Frick ordered as much steel armor produced as possible in preparation for the showdown. If the union wouldn't approve the pay cuts, he would shut the factory down and starve them out until they gave in. Frick locked down the factory, keeping out 1,100 workers. He announced he would not deal with the unions, but only individual workers. Workers tried to contact Carnegie, who had in the past gone on record defending the rights of labor. But Carnegie had gone on vacation and authorized Frick to do whatever he wanted to break down the union. Carnegie and Frick believed the workers would give up their union to hold onto their jobs. But it was not to be so easy.

While only 750 of the plant's 3,800 workers were members of the union, 3,000 of the workers met and decided by an overwhelming majority to strike. Frick responded by building a 12-foot fence around the factory. It was three miles in length with barbed wire on top and peepholes for putting rifles through. Workers called it "Fort Frick."

Deputy sheriffs were sworn in to protect the property. The workers chased them away and took over the factory. They believed they had invested themselves in the property through their labor and had some rights in regard to it. Frick was not about to honor any such right.

Frick hired the Pinkerton Detective Agency, which he had hired before, as his private army. On July 5, tugboats pulled barges up the Monongahela River carrying hundreds of Pinkertons with Winchester rifles to the Homestead factory. But workers spotted the approaching Pinkertons and a horseman rode into the streets of Homestead at 3 a.m. warning that the Pinkertons were coming. Thousands of strikers and sympathizers got out of bed and went down to the river to meet the private army.

The workers warned the Pinkertons not to disembark, but the warning was ignored. Shots were exchanged and the Pinkertons retreated to the barges. For the next 14 hours it was war. Strikers rolled a flaming freightcar into the barges. They threw dynamite out to sink the barges and poured oil on the water and tried to light it. When the Pinkertons surrendered in the afternoon, three

Pinkertons and as many as nine workers had been killed, or were dying. The workers declared victory, but the war was not over.

The governor of Pennsylvania ordered the state militia to take action. Using the latest rifles and Gatling guns, they took over the plant. Four months after going on strike, the workers were out of resources, depleted and defeated. They returned to work. The strike's leaders were charged with murder and 160 other workers were charged with other crimes. The strike committee was charged with treason. But juries were sympathetic to the strikers and would not convict any of them on any charge. Strikers were blacklisted, unable to work again, and the Carnegie company succeeded in breaking the union. Frick had proven that a corporation could break the strongest craft union in the country.

The incident damaged Carnegie's reputation as a benign employer, and also his peace of mind. Though he had given Frick carte blanche before he slipped away from the scene, Carnegie was shaken by the incident.

He wrote in a letter to British statesman William Gladstone, "This is the trial of my life (death's hand excepted). Such a foolish step — contrary to my ideals, repugnant to every feeling of my nature. Our firm offered all it could offer, even generous terms. Our other men had gratefully accepted them. They went as far as I could have wished, but the false step was made in trying to run the Homestead Works with new men. It is a test to which workingmen should not be subjected. It is expecting too much of poor men to stand by and see their work taken by others. . . The pain I suffer increases daily. The Works are not worth one drop of human blood. I wish they had sunk."

Six years later Carnegie returned to Homestead to dedicate a library, a concert hall, a swimming pool, bowling alleys, and a gymnasium. But the pain of Homestead stayed with him. In his autobiography he wrote, "No pangs remain of any wound received in my business career save that of Homestead."

Chapter Five:
The Twentieth Century

Working Class Heroes
Joe Hill - 1879-1915

Joe Hill was one of the few people who was ever killed for writing a song. Such is the power of music, and of an idea, that it is so dangerous it must be suppressed by any means possible. Joe Hill was born in 1879 in Sweden as Joel Emmanuel Hägglund. When he came to America he shortened his name to Joseph Hillström to make it easier for Americans to pronounce. His colleagues and co-workers shortened it further to simply Joe Hill.

Hill's father Olof had been a railroad conductor. He died at age 41 leaving the family in desperate straits. His mother kept the family together until she died in 1902. At that point Joe and his brother Paul moved to the U.S. Hill worked as a migrant laborer in New York City, Cleveland and on the west coast. He was in San Francisco, California, at the time of the 1906 earthquake.

He learned English in the early 1900s as he worked various jobs. He faced the troubles of working people daily, wrote songs about them and drew cartoons. Some of his songs put new lyrics to familiar melodies of the time.

In 1910 he joined the radical union the Industrial Workers of the World (IWW), whose members were known as "Wobblies," and which became known to the establishment as "America's damnable enemy." Joe Hill became the Wobblies' chief songwriter.

His best known songs are "The Preacher and the Slave", "The Tramp", "There is Power in a Union", "The Rebel Girl", and "Casey Jones—the Union Scab". Hill's songs served as engines for the IWW movement. The songs were scathing critiques of the brutal industrial capitalism of the day, but they were driven with the additional power of humor. The music not only communicated a powerful message, but also could lift morale, and bring large groups of people into synchronization. Joe Hill was enormously valuable to the labor movement, and conversely a bitter irritant to the plutocrats and capitalist bosses.

When Hill's wanderings took him to Park City, Utah, in 1914 he wandered into a mess he would never escape from. A man named John G. Morrison and his son Arling were murdered in their butcher shop by two armed intruders with their faces covered by red bandanas. Nothing was stolen, and since the elder Morrison had been a police officer, the investigating police at first assumed it was a crime of revenge over something that happened during Morrison's police career. Starting with people who had been arrested by Morrison, police arrested 12 suspects. Then suddenly Joe Hill became the prime suspect.

The evening of the murder Hill had gone to a doctor with a bullet wound. He said he had been shot by a rival in a competition for the affections of a woman. The doctor said that Hill had a pistol, though it was never found. A red bandana, however, was found in Hill's room. Hill denied the charge. He said his hands had been over his head when he was shot, and the hole in his coat four inches below the bullet wound in his back supported his claim. Four other people were treated for gunshot wounds in Park City that night. Hill didn't know Morrison. There was no robbery, so there was no motive. The prosecution brought in a dozen witnesses who said Hill resembled the killer, including Morrison's 13-year-od son Merlin. When the boy first saw Hill he said, "That's not him at all." But later he identified him as the murderer. Hill was convicted. An appeal to the Utah Supreme Court was unsuccessful. Hill's lawyer, Orrin Hilton, wrote, "The main thing the state had on Hill was that he was an IWW and therefore sure to be guilty. Hill tried to keep the IWW out of [the trial]... but the press fastened it upon him."

According to Hill's lawyer, the murder victim had been a prominent citizen and someone would have to be a scapegoat for the murder. The case became a major event. Even President Woodrow Wilson and Helen Keller called for clemency.

William Adler, who published a biography of Joe Hill called *The Man Who Never Died* in 2011, claims that the evidence points to one of the police's early suspects, Frank Z. Wilson as the real killer. Frank Z. Wilson was an alias of Magnus Olson, an ex-convict who had done time in the Utah state penitentiary. Wilson/Olson had been on a criminal rampage in the days and weeks before the killings. He had a huge criminal record, including time working as a henchman for Al Capone. Wilson was in the vicinity of the crime scene at the time of the killings and he fit the profile of a murderer. The case against him was much stronger than the very thin circumstantial case used to convict Hill. Hill had no criminal history. But he did resemble Frank Z. Wilson. Other than that, the most damning evidence the police found on Hill was his red membership card for IWW.

Adler concludes that "Hill was almost certainly railroaded to his death by the powers that be in Utah, which saw him as a prized prisoner of the class war." Adler found a letter from Hilda

Erickson, the woman Hill was involved with, corroborating his story of how he got shot in the back. Hill did not testify at his own trial, which was considered suspicious by his accusers. He would not name the man who shot him or the woman who was at the center of the argument. Adler believes that Hill had come to see himself as more valuable to the labor movement as a dead martyr than a living songwriter.

He was killed by firing squad. His last words were, "Fire!" Just before his death, he wrote to IWW leader Bill Haywood saying, "Goodbye Bill. I die like a true blue rebel. Don't waste any time in mourning. Organize... Could you arrange to have my body hauled to the state line to be buried? I don't want to be found dead in Utah."

His last will and testament was characteristically in verse. It was later set to music by Ethel Raim, founder of the group The Pennywhistlers.

My will is easy to decide,
For there is nothing to divide.
My kin don't need to fuss and moan,
"Moss does not cling to a rolling stone."

My body? Oh, if I could choose
I would to ashes it reduce,
And let the merry breezes blow,
My dust to where some flowers grow.

Perhaps some fading flower then
Would come to life and bloom again.
This is my Last and final Will.
Good Luck to All of you,

Working Class Heroes

Big Bill Haywood 1869-1928

William D. or "Big Bill" Haywood was born in Salt Lake City when Utah was still a territory. His father was a Pony Express rider who died of pneumonia when Bill was three years old. An injury while he was whittling a slingshot when he was nine left him with a glass eye. Because of it, he always turned his head for the camera to show his left profile. He was only nine years old when he went to work in the mines. He received little formal education.

For a while he worked as a cowboy, but then returned to the mines. The stories about big news events, such as the destruction of the Molly Maguires, the Haymarket Incident in Chicago and the Pullman Strike in 1894 aroused his interest in the labor movement. When Ed Boyce, the president of the Western Federation of Miners spoke in 1896 at the silver mine where Haywood was working, he became inspired and signed on as a union member.

He threw himself into work for the union and by 1902 had become its second in command as secretary-treasurer of the WFM. That year the union was heavily engaged in struggles in the Cripple Creek mining district, struggles that went on for years and took the lives of 33 workers both union and non-union. The union launched a series of strikes in opposition to harsh working conditions and poverty wages. The strikes were failures in achieving their objectives and it convinced Haywood that larger unions that cut across different categories of labor within an industry were necessary to be able to hope to effectively oppose corporate power.

In 1904 Haywood joined with other radical labor leaders in Chicago to write a manifesto and declare a new union that could potentially unite more workers than anything before. It was named the Industrial Workers of the World. In June of 1905, a group met in Chicago to kick off the new organization. Haywood addressed the crowd, saying, "Fellow Workers, this is the Continental Congress of the working-class. We are here to confederate the workers of this country into a working-class movement that shall have for its purpose the emancipation of the working-class from the slave bondage of capitalism. The aims and objects of this organization shall be to put the working-class in possession of the economic power, the means of life, in control of the machinery of production and distribution, without regard to capitalist masters."

Also speaking at the convention were Eugene Debs and Mother Mary Jones. But events later that year would cause Haywood's career to take a sharp detour. On December 30, 1905, Frank Steunenberg, was killed by an explosion in front of his home. Steunenberg had been an enemy of the WFM, so suspicion fell upon the union. Authorities arrested Harry Orchard, the bodyguard of WFM President Charles Moyer. James McParland, the Pinkerton detective who had infiltrated and helped to destroy the Molly Maguires was put in charge of the case.

McParland ordered Orchard be put on death row, kept under surveillance and given limited rations. Then he brought Orchard into a meeting over a big lunch finished off with cigars and told Orchard the only way for him to escape hanging was to implicate the leaders of the WFM in the crime. He offered Orchard money and other benefits and managed to get a confession out of him for a number of murders. McParland used fake extradition papers to gain legal authority to cross state lines to capture three WFM leaders. The papers falsely stated that WFM leaders had been at the scene of the Steunenberg murder. In the operation Haywood, Moyer and George Pettibone were abducted, forced into a special train and literally railroaded out of the state before there was time for Colorado courts to respond to the extradition request.

Haywood was represented by the famous lawyer Clarence Darrow. The prosecution had no other evidence than that obtained from Orchard, a confessed bomber and murderer who admitted working for and taking money from both sides in the labor struggles. Haywood was acquitted. The trial made him famous and he was seen as a champion of labor. Eugene Debs called him "The Lincoln of Labor." He was known for blunt, memorable phrases. "The capitalist has no heart," he once said. "But harpoon him in his pocketbook and you will draw blood."

In January 1912, 20,000 textile workers in Lawrence, Massachusetts, walked off their jobs to protest pay cuts. The IWW took the responsibility for leading of the strike. The police were called to crack down on the strike and violence erupted. Local IWW leaders were imprisoned for the murder of Anna LoPizzo, one of the strikers, though 19 witnesses said the striker had been killed by police gunfire. Martial Law was declared. Haywood went to the scene with other organizers to supervise the strike closely. Haywood introduced a number of innovative techniques as the strike continued week after week. One of the tactics was to send the hungry children of strikers to live with sympathizers in neighboring states. Haywood had heard of the tactic being used during prolonged strikes in Europe. The IWW advertised in socialist newspapers to find sympathetic families who would be willing to help. As the first group of strikers' children bid farewell to their parents to board a train for New York, it attracted attention, popular sympathy and confusion from establishment politicians in Massachusetts, who were suddenly embarrassed by the plight of the children.

Authorities tried to stop the notorious exoduses of children, sending police to forcibly separate children from their mothers, setting off a wild, violent scene, and imprisoning many workers and their children. It became a national scandal leading to congressional hearings and the bad publicity forced the mill owners to agree to the workers' demands.

Haywood was Marxist in his political views, and was an active member in the Socialist Party for many years. In 1912 he was elected to the party's National Executive Committee. But his aggressiveness and his call for abolishing the wage system and overthrowing capitalism made more moderate members of the Socialist party nervous. Haywood and the IWW had little interest in electoral politics and preferred direct action, which often led to violence. When Haywood stated his preference for direct action during a speech in New York the State Executive Committee of the Socialist Party of New York launched an initiative to remove Haywood from the national committee. His recall was approved two to one. He left the Socialist Party and thousands of IWW members and sympathizers went with him.

During the Paterson Silk Strike of 1913, Haywood and the IWW staged a Paterson Strike Pageant at Madison Square Garden. Actual strikers appeared and acted out the strike. The move was so novel it made Haywood a celebrity among progressives and intellectuals.

But his heyday was to be short lived. The onset of World War I led to the passing of the Espionage Act of 1917. It was originally meant to stop anyone from interfering in a military operation, but its use was widened. Eugene V. Debs was sentenced to 10 years in prison for an antiwar speech that was claimed to have "obstructed recruiting" by speaking against the war. The Department of Justice, with the approval of President Woodrow Wilson, arrested 165 IWW members for "conspiring to hinder the draft, encourage desertion, and intimidate others in connection with labor disputes."

In April 1918 Haywood went on trial with 100 other IWW members and all were convicted. Haywood and 14 others were given 20 year sentences. Haywood tried unsuccessfully to overturn the conviction. Then when he was out on bail, he skipped the country. He went to Russia and was given a job as a labor advisor to the new Bolshevik government under Lenin. When Lenin died and Stalin took power, Haywood lost his job as an advisor. He lived his final days in Russia. Visitors in those years describe him as depressed and wishing he could return to America. Haywood died of a stroke in a Moscow hospital on May 18, 1928.

The Ludlow Massacre 1913-14

On April 20, 1914, the attention of the world was drawn to the burning of 11 children and two women in the Ludlow tent colony near the coal mines in southern Colorado.

Coal had been discovered in the late 1800s under the Rockies in Southern Colorado, formed by millions of years of pressure of the great weight of the Rocky Mountains. Railroads extended their lines from northern Colorado and New Mexico to meet at the mining area and a mining town was developed called Trinidad. The Colorado Fuel and Iron Corporation and other mining companies drilled into the mountains, advertised for workers and lowered them from 200 to 400 feet below the surface to bring the coal out of the earth. In darkness they hacked away at seams of coal with hand picks, loaded it into railroad cars that were hauled through mining shafts by mules, then lifted to the surface.

Workers were forced to live in little camps that were ruled like feudal kingdoms. They lived in makeshift huts and shanties cobbled together with newspapers and whatever material was available to block the winds. Workers were ruled with an iron hand. They lived under curfews. Visitors from outside were tightly screened. They were forced to buy their supplies at the company store.

The rules were enforced by marshals hired by the coal corporation. The teachers, preachers and doctors for the community were selected by the corporation. In 1902, John D. Rockefeller bought the Colorado Fuel and Iron Corporation. In 1911 he turned over the operation to his son, John D. Rockefeller Jr., who instituted policy changes. Liquor became big business. By 1914, the company ran 27 mining camps, as well as the land, houses, saloons, schools, churches and stores.

A superintendant for the company wrote to John Jr. that the company "became notorious in many sections for their support of the liquor interests. They established saloons everywhere they could."

In 1913 the United Mine Workers union began trying to organize the miners of Trinidad. The union had unsuccessfully tried to lead a strike there a decade before. The union asked the owners to negotiate. They refused and hired the Baldwin-Felts Detective Agency to enforce order. Hundreds of deputies were sworn in by the sheriffs in Las Animas and Huerfano Counties.

On Saturday night, August 16, 1913 a union organizer named Gerald Lippiatt arrived in Trinidad. He walked through the crowds on Trinidad's main street and encountered two Baldwin-Felts detectives. Angry words were spoken and Lippiatt was shot and killed.

The detectives were arrested, but released on $10,000 bond. A coroner's jury was formed, consisting of the head of Wells Fargo, the cashier at the Trinidad National Bank, the president of the Sherman-Cosmer Mercantile Company, the manager of the Columbia hotel, and the owner of a chain of stores. John C. Baldwin, a gambler and saloon keeper, was the jury's foreman. There was conflicting testimony on what happened and the jury decided it was justifiable homicide.

The incident fueled more union organizing and the corporation responded by importing hundreds of men under Baldwin-Felts. They brought in men from the saloons of Denver and others from outside the state to break the coming strike. More than

300 men were deputized by the sheriff and on the payroll of the coal company.

The miners union held a convention and miners registered their complaints. They said they were robbed on each ton of coal, beaten or fired for complaints, forced to vote in compliance with their bosses and constantly terrorized by armed guards.

Mother Jones, spoke at the convention. She told the crowd, "What would the coal in these mines and in these hills be worth unless you put your strength and muscle in to bring them?" She roused the crowds with a long, passionate speech. "Liberty is not dead," she said. "She is only quietly resting, waiting for you to call."

When the company refused to negotiate, the workers called a strike for September 23. Eleven thousand miners gathered their families and moved out of the company camp to new colonies set up by the union outside of the grounds. The largest camp was Ludlow, a railroad stop a few miles out of Trinidad. A thousand people, including nearly 300 children, lived in 400 tents there.

The company sent a specially armored car in with a gatling gun, a machine gun, mounted on top. It was called the Death Special. It attacked one of the tent colonies, killed a man and left a boy with 11 bullets in his leg. Armed guards marched 49 strikers to Trinidad with the Death Special pointing its gun at their backs to force them back to work. A number of violent confrontations broke out. A steel-covered railroad car with 190 guards armed with rifles and machine guns headed to Ludlow. It met a group of armed miners and a skirmish ensued that left one guard dead. The guards kept machine guns and searchlights trained on the tents. A state of siege continued for weeks. The governor declared a state of martial law. He prohibited more strike breaking forces to be imported from outside the state and ordered the National Guard into the strike zone. The strikers hoped that the troops would moderate between the opposing sides, enforce the rule of law. A thousand of them, wasting away from starvation, lined up to greet the troops, some holding banners they had improvised for the occasion. But the troops proceeded to crack down harshly on the strikers. The miners responded with violence of their own, on a smaller scale. Tensions built, violence escalated, and on April 20, the National Guard exploded two dynamite bombs as a signal for an assault to begin. A machine gun began firing into the tents. Women tried to escape with their children. Several men were killed trying to get to the women to help them.

Lieutenant Linderfeldt, head of the National Guard contingent, sent word he wanted to meet with the strike leader, a man named Tikas. At first Tikas refused, then agreed. He carried a white flag to meet Linderfeldt on the hill. The only witness was an engineer, who said he saw the two men talking, then Linderfeldt brought his rifle down on Tikas' head with enough force to break it in two. Tikas fell forward and the militia men aimed their rifles at the unconscious man and shot him to death. Two other unarmed strikers were killed in the same way. The guardsmen kept up their attack until they finally "captured" the colony, or what was left of it. Twenty six bodies of strikers were found.

The New York Times reported grisly details of the massacre and it ignited a wave of anger. More strikers gathered from other colonies and for a while it was a war, with a series of skirmishes. Word of the state of siege spread and demonstrations were held around the country in support of the miners, attracting high-profile demonstrators like Upton Sinclair, author of *The Jungle,* who picketed Rockefeller's office in New York. President Woodrow Wilson called in troops to restore order. For seven months there was talk of negotiations and plans of mediation, but nothing happened. After seven months the strike petered out. The union had not achieved recognition. Sixty-six men, women and children had been killed. No militiamen or guards were ever indicted for a crime. In spite of a noble effort, the uprising was crushed.

The Great Depression

The Great Depression left many homeless and jobless, threw the country into a state of widespread economic standstill. Large groups of people traveled the country without homes, jobs, income or sufficient food. It set the stage for social unrest.

In 1932 New York Governor Franklin D. Roosevelt ran against President Herbert Hoover as a populist, and seized on the issues that were igniting anger across the country, including the concentration of capital and control in a few hands. Six hundred companies controlled two thirds of American industry, he said. "If the process of concentration goes on at the same rate, at the end of another century we shall have all American industry controlled by a dozen corporations, and run by perhaps a hundred men. Put plainly, we are steering a steady course toward economic oligarchy, if we are not there already."

Roosevelt defeated Hoover by seven million votes. In his first 100 days in office he pushed through a flurry of legislation to stimulate the economy, and the Supreme Court struck down one measure after another, even as the new programs were succeeding in getting the country's economy moving again, and put people back to work. Frustrated, Roosevelt asked Congress for the authority to appoint a new Supreme Court Justice for everyone who had passed the age of 70 and not retired. It would have given him the power to appoint six judges. The idea was rejected by the Senate, but the court did shift and began to allow policies that were supported by a large majority to take effect. One of the justices, Owen Roberts, shifted to the Roosevelt side, giving that side a one-vote majority. Roberts said that he shifted to supporting Roosevelt's laws out of concern about the spreading social unrest and the fear that if the Roosevelt policies were blocked, even more radical activities may prevail.

Auto-Lite Strike (1934)

In the 1930s there were many strikes that gradually transformed the political landscape. One of the first was a strike against Electric Auto-Lite in Toledo, Ohio. Union members demanded recognition of their union and a 10 percent wage increase. The owners countered with an offer of a five percent increase and a commitment to negotiate later in the year. When no contract emerged, the workers went on strike. By the time the strike had been going on a month, more than 10,000 demonstrated. Sheriff's deputies arrested and beat workers. Street fighting broke out between police and strikers. Workers pulled a fire hose from police and turned it back on them. When police started using tear gas, strikers threw bricks and stones at the Auto-Lite factory, set police cars on fire and used inner tubes as slingshots. Fifty-three out of 103 unions voted for a general strike. The strike succeeded in securing the full 10 percent wage increase and recognition of the union. It also led to a movement toward increased unionization in Toledo.

The National Labor Relations Act of 1935

On July 5, 1935 President Roosevelt signed the National Labor Relations Act, which put into law protections for unions and working people and formally recognized the right to collective bargaining. It protected their right to join together for mutual assistance, to form or join labor unions and bargain collectively for wages or working conditions. It prohibited employers with interfering with these rights or discriminating against workers who engaged in union organizing or activities. After a century and a half of bitter struggle, unions had achieved legal status in the US.

The Court Shifts

In the late 1930s, the court began to change its tack and started upholding the same kinds of social legislation it had so often overturned. The turning point was the 1937 West Coast Hotel Company v. Parrish case, in which the court upheld a Washington state law that set a minimum wage for women and children.

The shift in the ideological stance of the Supreme Court reflected the changing times. In the 1930s, after the stock market crash of 1929, the country was deeply enmired in the Great Depression. By 1933 industrial production was down 50 percent. Unemployment was 25 percent. Two million people wandered the country looking for any kind of work they could find to keep body and soul intact. More than 25,000 veterans and their families went to Washington to demand that the government pay early on bonuses that were promised them for serving in World War I. They set up camps made up of makeshift shacks and shanties and became known as the Bonus Army. Hoover sent the army in to clear out the veterans. Under the leadership of Douglas Macarthur, tanks and mounted soldiers marched on the veterans, attacked them with tear gas, drove them away and burned down their shacks.

Social unrest was spreading across the country, with wildcat strikes (not authorized by union leadership), riots and takeover of factories occurring frequently. The establishment began to see the organization of unions as preferable to the anarchy of explosions of blind rage of hungry, frustrated unemployed people. In 1932 Congress passed the Norris-LaGuardia act, which barred federal courts from issuing injunctions against nonviolent labor disputes and recognized the rights of workers to join unions.

The Roosevelt Legacy

In his last term, Roosevelt proposed a 'second bill of rights' guaranteeing a measure of financial security to Americans. It would guarantee the right to employment at an adequate wage, the right of farmers to a decent return on their products, the right of small businessmen to protection from predatory and monopolistic and unfair business practices, the right of families to own homes, the right to education and medical care and the right of the elderly, the disabled and the unemployed to some basic economic security. It was the culmination of a tendency that began in the 1600s and 1700s with the Enlightenment and the vision articulated by John Locke, Emile Jean-Jacques Rousseau and Voltaire, for the elevation of the individual rather than large institutions. Thomas Jefferson borrowed much of the language in The Declaration of Indepedence from John Locke's "Concerning Civil Government."

From Roosevelt's term through the 1960s, union rights were recognized as a legitimate part of American society. A relative balance of power remained in place and during that time the middle class strengthened beyond anything that had been seen before. A large part of the American population enjoyed a level of affluence and high standard of living beyond anything seen before. American prosperity at the time was due to a variety of factors. But the relatively equitable distribution

Franklin D. Roosevelt

of wealth could be attributed at least in some significant measure to the efforts over generations of the labor movement.

Liberal economist John Kenneth Galbraith, author of *The Affluent Society* and *The New Industrial State*, a Harvard professor and economic adviser to Roosevelt, Harry S. Truman, John F. Kennedy and Lyndon B. Johnson, thought the economic system had reached a self-regulating balance, that the expansion of corporate power automatically triggers and equal and opposite reaction in an assertion of power by labor. "Private economic power is held in check by the countervailing power of those who are subject to it,' he said. But as in all things in history, it seems, in the words of William Butler Yeats, 'things fall apart, the center cannot hold."

Working Class Heroes

John L. Lewis 1880-1969

John L. Lewis

John L. Lewis was a major force in the labor struggles with the mining industry throughout the first half of the 20th Century. Born in 1880 he served as president of the United Mine Workers for 40 years, from 1920 to 1960. He was one of the founders and the first president of the Congress of Industrial Organizations, which also created the United Steel Workers and organized millions of industrial workers in industries across America.

He was the embodiment of an indomitable will, a cunning negotiator and tough fighter who won wage increases for his membership with aggressive tactics. He is credited with building the CIO into an organization that rivaled the AFL to the extent that they finally merged into the AFL-CIO.

The son of Welsh immigrants, Lewis was born in Lucas, Iowa. His father was a coal miner. Lewis joined his father in the mines when he was 16. He became the recording secretary of UMWA (United Mine Workers of America) local 1933 and then in 1901 went west, rode the rails and experienced the life of the laborer. In 1905 he returned to Iowa and married Myrta Bell and they moved to Panama, Ill. He was elected president of UMWA local 1475. He lobbied the state legislature for workers' compensation and mine safety legislation and came to the attention of Samuel Gompers, then president of the AFL, who invited him to join as a national organizer and field representative. He worked for the AFL from 1910 to 1916, while also working closely with the president of the UMWA, John White, who offered him a job as international statistician of the UMWA. His abilities as an analyst were soon overshadowed by his abilities as a negotiator and he became the principal driving force of the union's leadership. As the country went into World War I and wartime regulations on labor-management relations came into effect, Lewis skillfully navigated through the new regulations to gain wage increases for miners. He became vice president in 1919 and then took over as president in 1920.

At the age of 40 he now led the most powerful union in the country.

In the 1920s when the country was very dependent on coal energy for rail transportation and heat, he lobbied for federal regulation to stabilize the industry, so the entire industry would not be crippled by the boom-and-bust production cycle of an unregulated industry.

Though raised in a Republican family, he found the Democratic party more receptive to the needs of working people after Franklin Roosevelt was elected in 1932. He made the union a powerful force in Roosevelt's landslide re-election victory in 1936. Later he broke with Roosevelt over the President's involving the U.S. in World War II.

Lewis became disillusioned with the ability of the AFL leadership to really organize workers and led an assault on the leadership at the 1935 AFL convention, demanding they fulfill their promises to organize industrial unions. His initiatives were defeated, but he provoked a confrontation in which he leaped over a row of chairs to floor the president of the carpenters union with a punch in the face and earned himself notoriety as a champion of working people. Capitalizing on his new fame, he committed the funds of the UMWA to organizing drives in the auto, rubber and steel industries, becoming instrumental in the success of the campaigns. He worked closely with the campaigns and personally negotiated deals with General Motors and US Steel.

The Congress of Industrial Organizations (CIO) held its founding convention in 1938 and Lewis was elected its first president. Lewis' inspiring oratory and his bold demands on corporate power earned him a broad following. He became known as the conscience of American industry and the face of the labor movement.

But in 1940 he broke with Roosevelt over the President's war policies and pledged his support to the Republican challenger. The rank-and-file membership stayed with Roosevelt and Lewis resigned as president of the CIO. In 1940, he broke with the CIO formally and pulled the UMWA out of it. He then focused again on the coal industry and led the UMWA through strikes in 1943 and 1946. As coal was gradually replaced by oil as the nation's number one energy source, he fought to maintain employment security for miners. He helped to engineer a historic deal that provided medical and pension benefits to miners in 1948. In the 1950s he continued to win wage increases for members and led the campaign for the Federal Mine Safety Act of 1952. He retired from the UMWA in 1960 and died in 1969.

World War II

Post-World War II Servicemen's Strike Wave (1945)

Franklin D. Roosevelt's efforts to generate enough economic activity to pull the country out of depression and put people back to work were stalled by obstacles put in his way by reactionary forces on the Supreme Court and elsewhere. But with the U.S. entry into World War II, all obstacles were pulled out of the way of the war effort, and it generated enough economic activity to finally pull the country into economic health. At the end of the war the New Deal was well established and had become accepted as a successful way to manage the economic system of a country and to produce the most prosperity and well being for the most people. The liberalism of the New Deal became the dominant philosophy of government. The Democrats held majorities in both houses of Congress.

General Eisenhower, the Supreme Allied Commander who had led the Invasion of Normandy and the liberation of Europe from the Nazis, was elected president as a Republican, but he was elected because of his extreme popularity as a war leader, not because of the popularity of the Republican philosophy. The political climate in Washington continued to be dominated by New Deal politics through the '60s and early '70s, so much so that Nixon, who had first been elected to political office by fraudulently smearing opponents as Communists, ended up passing some of the most liberal and anti-corporate programs in American history, such as environmental protection and workplace health and safety laws.

But nothing in history is static and even as pro-democracy reforms in the New Deal style were reaching their apex under Nixon, the ground was already being prepared for a new conservative reign. Many of the purveyors of the neoconservative movement were nurtured in the Nixon White House, including George Bush, Dick Cheney, Karl Rove, Pat Buchanan and others.

WORKING CLASS HEROES:
George Meany (1894-1980)

George Meany was the most nationally recognized labor leader in America for two decades in mid-20th Century, from 1955 to 1979. He was president of the American Federation of Labor (AFL) from 1952 to 1955, then pushed for the merger of the AFL and Congress of Industrial Organizations (CIO) and took charge in managing that merger.

He was born in Harlem, New York City, in 1894 to Irish Catholic parents. His Irish ancestors had immigrated to the U.S. in the 1850s. His father was a plumber and a dedicated union member. George grew up in the Bronx, dropped out of high school at age 16 and became an apprentice plumber for a five-year stint. His father died suddenly of a heart attack in 1916, and when his brother joined the army in 1917, George was the sole support for his mother and her six younger children. For a while he played semi-professional baseball on top of his work as a plumber.

In 1920 he was elected to the executive board of local 463 of his union, the United Association of Plumbers and Steamfitters of the United States and Canada. He became the union's full-time business agent. He was elected secretary of the New York City Building Trades Council in 1923 and won an injunction against a lockout in 1927, which was an innovative tactic for unions at the time. In 1934 he became president of the New York State Federation of Labor. He became a spokesman for the labor movement because of his ability to speak clearly to the press or in legislative hearings. He was a co-founder of the American Labor Party in 1936, which campaigned for Franklin Roosevelt's re-election.

In 1939 he became secretary-treasurer of the AFL based in Washington DC. During World War II he was one of AFL's representatives on the National War Labor Board. He became aligned with anti-communist leaders of the labor movement and in 1945 led the AFL boycott of the World federation of Trade Unions, which had allowed Soviet communist labor groups to join.

When William Green, the president of the AFL, became ill in 1951, Meany gradually took over his day-to-day responsibilities, and became president in 1952 when Green died. Only a few days before Green died, the president of the CIO, Philip Murray, died, and many were calling for the merger of the two organizations. Walter Reuther had become president of the CIO and he supported the merger. So Meany's first official act as president was to propose the merger. It took three years to complete the merger. There was opposition from significant labor leaders, including John L. Lewis of the United Mine Workers and Jimmy Hoffa, second in command of the Teamsters Union.

In the mid-1950s concerns arose about the influence of organized crime on the International Brotherhood of Teamsters. There was a battle for power within the union between two factions, one led by Dave Beck and the other by Jimmy Hoffa. The concerns with corruption led Meany to launch an anti-corruption campaign in 1956. Beck was called before the U.S. Senate Select Committee on

Improper Activities in Labor and Management, known as the McClellan Committee. Misconduct of both Beck and Hoffa was revealed in the hearings and both were indicted. Hoffa managed to win control of the Teamsters from Beck. The AFL-CIO under Meany initiated a policy under which no union official who had pleaded the Fifth Amendment, exercised his right to remain silent before a congressional committee, could serve in a leadership role. That meant Hoffa. Meany said the Teamsters could continue in the AFL-CIO if Hoffa was ousted. The Teamsters refused so Meany kicked the union out of the AFL-CIO in late 1957. Meany moved for the adoption of a code of ethics for the AFL-CIO after the Teamsters scandal.

In 1965 under President Lyndon Johnson, Meany and the AFL-CIO endorsed a resolution calling for "mandatory congressional price hearings for corporations, a technological clearinghouse, and a national planning agency." He supported Johnson's military involvement in Vietnam and criticized labor leaders like Walter Reuther of the United Auto Workers who called for U.S. withdrawal from Vietnam. He believed a communist takeover of South Vietnam would destroy its free trade unions. Division in the country over the Vietnam War also infected the AFL-CIO and in 1967 when its convention adopted a resolution pledging support for the war effort, Charles Cogen, president of the American Federation of Teachers, opposed Meany for the presidency of the AFL-CIO. Meany continued his support for the war effort until the end. He disliked the antiwar movement and the New Left, and remained staunchly anti-communist and socially conservative. In 1979 he resigned from the AFL-CIO after a 57-year career in organized labor.

Working Class Heroes:
Walter Reuther 1907-1970

Walter Reuther was born in 1907 in Wheeling, West Virginia, the son of a socialist brewery worker who had immigrated from Germany. He joined Ford Motor Company in 1927 as an expert tool and die maker. In 1932 during the Great Depression he was laid off, and he claimed it was because of his socialist activities. He went with his brothers to Europe and got a job in an auto factory in Gorky, USSR, and became familiar with a different kind of work environment from what he had known. "The atmosphere of freedom and security, shop meetings with their proletarian industrial democracy, all these things make an inspiring contrast to what we know as Ford wage slaves in Detroit," he wrote. "What we have experienced here has reeducated us along new and practical lines."

He did not, however, like the lack of political freedom in the Soviet Union. He returned to the U.S., got a job with General Motors and joined the union, the United Automobile Workers (UAW). He joined the Socialist Party, had some dealings with the Communist Party and cooperated with them in the late 1930s as part of what was called the Popular Front. He agreed with them on practical matters of the union but was staunchly anti-Stalin. Impressed by Franklin Roosevelt's efforts to moderate capitalism, Reuther joined the Democratic party.

In 1936 he was elected president of local 174. He led several strikes during the next few years, was badly beaten by strike breakers, survived two assassination attempts and his right hand was crippled in an attack in 1948.

On May 26, 1937, the United Auto Workers launched a leaflet campaign at the overpass on Miller Road at the Ford plant in Dearborn, Michigan. The union was asking for a six-hour day at a pay scale of $8 instead of the current eight-hour day at $6. A newspaper photographer asked some of the UAW organizers to pose for a photo and while they were posing as many as 40 of Ford's internal security agents jumped them and started to beat them. "Seven times they raised me off the concrete and slammed me down on it," Reuther wrote. "They pinned my arms ... and I was punched and kicked and dragged by my feet to the stairway, thrown down the first flight of steps, picked up, slammed down on the platform and kicked down the second flight. On the ground they beat and kicked me some more..." One union organizer's back was broken during the attack. The goons beat women handing out leaflets and reporters and photographers while police stood by passively. The agents tried to destroy the photographic plates, but the Detroit News photographer hid them and turned over blanks instead. Later the photographs were published along with a report of the attack. The photographs of the attack inspired the Pulitzer committee to create a prize for photography. The head of Ford's security force said, "The affair was deliberately provoked by union officials. . . . They simply wanted to trump up a charge of Ford brutality. ... I know definitely no Ford service man or plant police were involved in any way in the fight." But the incident aroused support for the UAW and hurt Ford's reputation. Ford and its security chief were chastised by the National Labor Relations Board and three years later Ford signed a contract with the UAW.

As a senior organizer, Reuther helped to win major strikes for union recognition against General Motors in 1940 and Ford in 1941. But he supported the war effort after the onset of World War II and refused to tolerate wildcat strikes that could disrupt weapons production. But after the war was over he led a 113-day strike against General Motors, which achieved wage increases, but not the power sharing arrangement he was seeking. In 1946 he was elected head of the UAW and led a purge of communist elements from the organization. He was also active in the CIO at the time and became president of it in 1952. He negotiated a merger of the CIO with the AFL under George Meany in 1955.

Reuther managed to win advantageous contracts for his members through skilled negotiating. He would target one of the Big Three automakers at a time. If it would not grant the concession he was seeking, he would lead a strike that would allow the other two automakers to capture some of its marketshare. He won raises in pay, paid vacations, employer funded pensions (beginning in 1950 with Chrysler), medical insurance (beginning with GM in 1950) and supplementary unemployment benefits (starting with Ford in 1955).

Buckminster Fuller, the inventor of the geodesic dome and a union machinist, said Reuther, as head of the UAW, fed data into a computer to ask the question: Which will make General Motors more money, to grant or not to grant shorter hours, higher pay, vacation time and health and retirement benefits to its employees? The computer answered that it would make more money by granting. Fuller thought that Reuther probably showed his results to the GM brass because they granted his request with uncharacteristically light resistance. Within three years of granting the benefits, GM became the first corporation to make a $1 billion after taxes. “This is how well it paid off to allow a percentage of accrued profits to fund labor’s wider buying power,” said Fuller. “They made money because mass production cannot exist without mass consumption, and the wider and more persistent the distribution of wealth as buying power, the greater and more persistent the sales and profits to all. General Motors’ decision to heed the computers insured their profits.”

In his later life he remained an activist, strongly supporting the Civil Rights movement and participating in the March on Washington for Freedom and Jobs in 1963 and the Selma to Montgomery March in 1965. He stood next to Martin Luther King during the "I Have A Dream" speech at the 1963 March on Washington. Though he was critical of the Vietnam War, he remained an ally of President Johnson, meeting with him weekly in 1964 and 1965, and he supported Hubert Humphrey for president in 1968.

Reuther and his brother Victor were almost killed in a small private plane that crashed in October 1968 as it approached Dulles Airport in Washington DC. In May 1970 Reuther was again in a plane crash and that time he was killed. Years after the crash his brother said in an interview, "I and other family members are convinced that both the fatal crash and the near fatal one in 1968 were not accidental." The FBI still refuses to turn over nearly 200 pages of documents pertaining to Reuther's death, and the correspondence between field offices and J. Edgar Hoover.

Reuther was chosen by Time magazine for its list of the 100 most influential people of the 20th Century. In 1995, he was posthumously awarded the Presidential Medal of Freedom by President Bill Clinton.

Chapter Six:

The Decline of Unions and the Conservative Resurgence

In the 1960s the people's movement was in ascendancy. Significant progress was made for the Civil Rights movement. The antiwar movement succeeded in stopping the American military action in Southeast Asia. The women's movement was blossoming. And force was gathering for environmental protection. These were all pro-democracy movements, which had the effect of expanding the democratic franchise, enacting the will and serving the interests of the majority and threatened the power and the principal interests of Corporate America.

In just two years, 1969 and 1970, seven major consumer and environmental organizations were formed: Friends of the Earth, Common Cause, Environmental Action, the Center for Law and Social Policy, the Consumer Federation of America, Public Citizen and the Natural Resources Defense Council. The momentum gathered quickly and caught corporate America unprepared, and unable to ward off a flurry of regulatory legislation, including the National Environmental Protection Act in 1969, the Clean Air Act Amendments in 1970, the banning of cigarette commercials from radio and television and the cancellation of funding for the Supersonic Transport Plane in 1970.

Corporations Join Forces

In 1971 Lewis Powell Jr., a board member of Philip Morris and 10 other corporate boards, wrote a confidential memorandum addressed to the U.S.Chamber of Commerce that came to be known as the Powell Memo. It had an enormous effect on the progression of history in the United States, especially on the struggle between corporate and democratic power. The Powell Memo, entitled "Attack on American Free Enterprise System," was in effect a manifesto for Corporate America for its takeover of the country. The attack on the free enterprise system that Powell referred to was the rise of regulations and restrictions on what corporations could do that had been put in place since President Franklin Roosevelt's New Deal in the 1930s. It started with Roosevelt, but the trend was sustained through the following presidents: Truman, Eisenhower, Kennedy, Johnson, and Nixon.

Lewis Powell

During that period, working people made tremendous strides. The middle class had grown. The country was economically strong and the wealth was spread around. Regulations were put on the banks, to help stop the corrupt practices that had always led to periodic depressions. Unions were empowered to represent workers. Companies were required to provide benefits and better working conditions. Minimum wage requirements were put in place. Social Security was established under Roosevelt, Medicare under Johnson. In the 1970s when Nixon was president, companies were prevented from dumping toxic waste wherever they wanted to. They Occupational Safety and Health regulations were put in place and corporations were required to fulfill them. To Powell and his conservative brethren, all this constituted an attack on the free enterprise system itself.

The Powell Memo laid out a plan of attack for Corporate America to seize back lost ground. Two months after Powell wrote the memo, President Nixon nominated Powell to the Supreme Court, where he would have great power to put his beliefs into effect through the nation's legal system. Bill Moyers said of the Powell Memo, "We look back on it now as a call to arms for class war waged from the top down."

Powell led a rallying by the business community, and a conscious recognition that Corporate America had to band together to fight back against the encroachment of the democratic and peoples movements. In his paper, he wrote, "Strength lies in organization, in careful long-range planning and implementation, in the scale of financing available only through joint effort, and in the political power available through united action and national organizations."

Powell believed only a combined effort could save the objectives of Corporate America. "The day is long past when the chief executive officer of a major corporation discharges his responsibility by maintaining a satisfactory growth of profits... If our system is to survive, top management must be equally concerned with protecting and preserving the system itself."

Powell outlined a plan of attack that included spreading the conservative message through public speaking campaigns; taking on major organs of public opinions like universities, media and the courts; keeping TV programs and school textbooks under "constant surveillance" and staying on the attack whenever their message was in defiance of the conservative message; aggressively working for advantage within the political system; setting up think tanks, foundations and front groups to push conservative values throughout society. He saw the U.S.Chamber of Commerce as a war council within which the chieftains of industry could wage a unified campaign. Results would not be immediate, but, he wrote, the desired results would eventually come from "careful long-range planning and implementation, in consistency of action over an indefinite period of years, in the scale of financing available only through joint effort, and in the political power available only through united action and united organizations."

Through Powell the awareness spread through the kingpins of business in Corporate America, that they would have to band together consciously to save their system from being broken down and their power eroded by democratic action on behalf of people's issues. Corporate America realized that its biggest threat was from democracy itself. And the biggest agents on behalf of the public's interest were the unions and other grassroots reform organizations.

Within two years of Powell's writing of the memo, the U.S. Chamber of Commerce set up a task force of 40 executives from major corporations, including U.S. Steel, GE, GM, Phillips Petroleum, 3M, Amway, and ABC and CBS. The latter two were officially organs of the free press, but they were also major corporations and shared the objectives of other major corporations. The task force led the charge to put Powell's plan into effect. The National Association of Manufacturers moved its main offices from New York to Washington. In 1971, 175 companies had registered lobbyists in Washington. In 1982, the number was up to nearly 2,500. The number of corporate PACs increased from fewer than 300 in 1976 to more than 1,200 by the mid 1980s. Foundations were formed to further the cause, including The American Legislative Exchange Council (ALEC), the Heritage Foundation, the Cato Institute, the Manhattan Institute, Citizens for a Sound Economy (later renamed Americans for Prosperity) and the Business Roundtable.

The Business Roundtable

The new consciousness of corporate solidarity set off a new wave of political organizing in the business community. In 1972 Frederick Borch of General Electric and John Harper of Alcoa led the formation of a new organization of CEOs from the top 200 financial, industrial and service organizations. The Business Roundtable formed a supercorporate legislative body that wielded substantial influence from the beginning by virtue of the elite status of its members. It gave big business a stronger, more focused platform from which to influence political events than anything previously seen. The major corporate and financial powers already shared many interests in common and tended to move in unison on a broad front of issues. But as a unified whole now consciously united behind a common agenda, they were able to wield a new measure of power.

This new level of power of corporate America and the success of the Business Roundtable was illustrated vividly in 1977 when a union-backed proposal to reform labor law and repeal some right-to-work provisions of the Taft Hartley act gained momentum in Congress. The corporate elite had varying attitudes toward the bill. Some, like Sears and Roebuck opposed the bill because it might encourage its labor force to unionize. Other companies that were already unionized, such as General Electric and General Motors, were unconcerned about the bill because it would have little effect on their businesses. But after the Business Roundtable voted to oppose the bill, all members jumped on the lobbying effort to oppose the bill.

In the wake of the success of the Business Roundtable the corporate and financial elites began to form a plethora of policy institutes, foundations, think tanks, lobbying and PR agencies and publications to support the corporate agenda. The propaganda effort kicked into high gear with plenty of money to invest in the most sophisticated advertising and public relations efforts ever developed.

Major corporate barons heard the call and went beyond the call of duty to participate in effort to move forward the corporate agenda. Joseph Coors, the beer magnate, was inspired by Powell's memo to set aside $250,000 as a donation to the Analysis and Research Association, which was later renamed the Heritage Foundation ...

The Powell memo also inspired the California Chamber of Commerce to form the Pacific Legal Foundation, the first of eight conservative litigation centers formed as a "counterintelligentsia" to help business shore up its ideological foundation, according to William Simon, the treasury secretary under Nixon, head of the Olin Foundation and one of the funders and supporters of the conservative legal effort.

The American Legislative Exchange Council was founded in 1973 originally to campaign on right wing morality issues such as anti-abortion rights and pro-school prayer. But later it found a fruitful alliance with the corporate sector. As major corporations donated to the association, it became more and more opportune for the association to cater to their interests and fight for their issues as well. The association grew until its corporate members numbered 300. It presented itself as a provider of technical office services to legislators, but it had a particular forte for writing bills that were cleverly titled by PR specialists to sound much more benign than they really were, such as The Environmental Good Samaritan Act and the Property Protection. Incorporating a good PR pitch into the language of the law has become an essential part of the art of crafting legislation.

The Corporate Agenda and Strategies

Building on its tremendous successes in the public relations field, Corporate America launched a barrage of assaults to further the corporate agenda through the power of public relations and marketing. There was little restraint on the basis of decorum or ethics. Smears and dirty tricks were an important part of the political PR arsenal. To discredit and smear an environmental protection advocacy group, Hill & Knowlton distributed a memo on the association's letterhead advocating violence "to fuck up the mega-machine."

Another technique that became known as "astroturfing" involved creating shell organizations that appeared to be powered by grassroots support, but were actually fronts for corporate advocacy under false pretenses.

With their superior capital strength, major corporations could also intimidate opponents into silence and inaction with lawsuits. Even a lawsuit with no basis can tie up major funds in legal expenses for a small organization and bankrupt it.

In 1996, Oprah Winfrey had a guest on her TV show who discussed the fact that American beef producers were feeding cows to other cows, that is putting dead cow parts into processed livestock feed, a practice that had previously led to an outbreak of mad cow disease in Britain. The Animal Industry Foundation sued for slander. There is no slander in reporting an acknowledged fact, but though the suit had no merit, it cost Winfrey millions in legal fees.

Deregulation

Corporate America in the early '70s rallied against what it saw as the incursion of regulations and people's rights and united to form a formidable campaign to build political power for corporations and those who supported a corporate world order, a society in which corporate power ruled the land. The assault led Corporate America to an unprecedented ascendance in power over the lives and minds of millions of Americans.

But in the early '70s Corporate America was still restrained in how much it could use money to influence politics. Campaign finance reform had been enacted through The Tillman Act, which was passed under President Theodore Roosevelt in 1907. Roosevelt had called for campaign finance reform after he had been charged with accepting donations in return for access.

It was 40 years later that labor unions were also banned from making political donations under the Taft Hartley Act of 1947. It was the unions who devised the mechanism by which Corporate America would eventually get around the campaign finance restrictions. It was through the PAC, political action committee. PACs were a way union members could pool their money for political donations. Corporate PACs were made legal by the Federal Election Campaign Act in 1971 and 1974, but though the corporate board could solicit stockholders for money, it could not solicit employees. This restriction, however, was lifted in 1975 by a ruling of the Federal Election Commission. The SUN-PAC ruling gave corporations the right to solicit funds from employees for political donations and to use money from their corporate treasuries to operate the PACs.

Then in 1978 corporations and unions and wealthy individuals were given the right to donate money for "party building" activities as long as it was not directly used to influence federal elections. This became another way to funnel money into the political process peripherally, and it became known as "soft money."

In 2002 Enron, a giant corporation that wielded a heavy hand in Washington through political donations, came tumbling down in a scandal in which it became known that the company had defrauded nearly everyone in the process of building its empire. Enron had provided George W. Bush's private jet during his presidential campaign in 2000 and had given money to many of the major power wielders in the legislature. The rage provoked by the scandal helped create the political environment in which campaign finance regulations could be enacted. The McCain-Feingold act in the Senate and the similar Shays-Meehan bill in the House of Representatives were combined to create a campaign finance law that banned the use of soft money. But the corporate sector challenged campaign finance in a lawsuit that went to the Supreme Court. It was the conservative Supreme Court that had ruled to stop the counting of votes in Florida and appoint George Bush president in 2000, and its conservative majority was strengthened with two conservative appointments during Bush's term. The uber-conservative court handed down what became known as the Citizens United ruling, which said that Congress has no right to prohibit corporations from giving as much money as they want to influence politics.

The Reagan Revolution

The year 1980 marks the year of the election of Ronald Reagan and the beginning of what was called the Reagan Revolution, and in this case the political slogan still stands as a credible name for what Reagan's election means for the history of the United States.

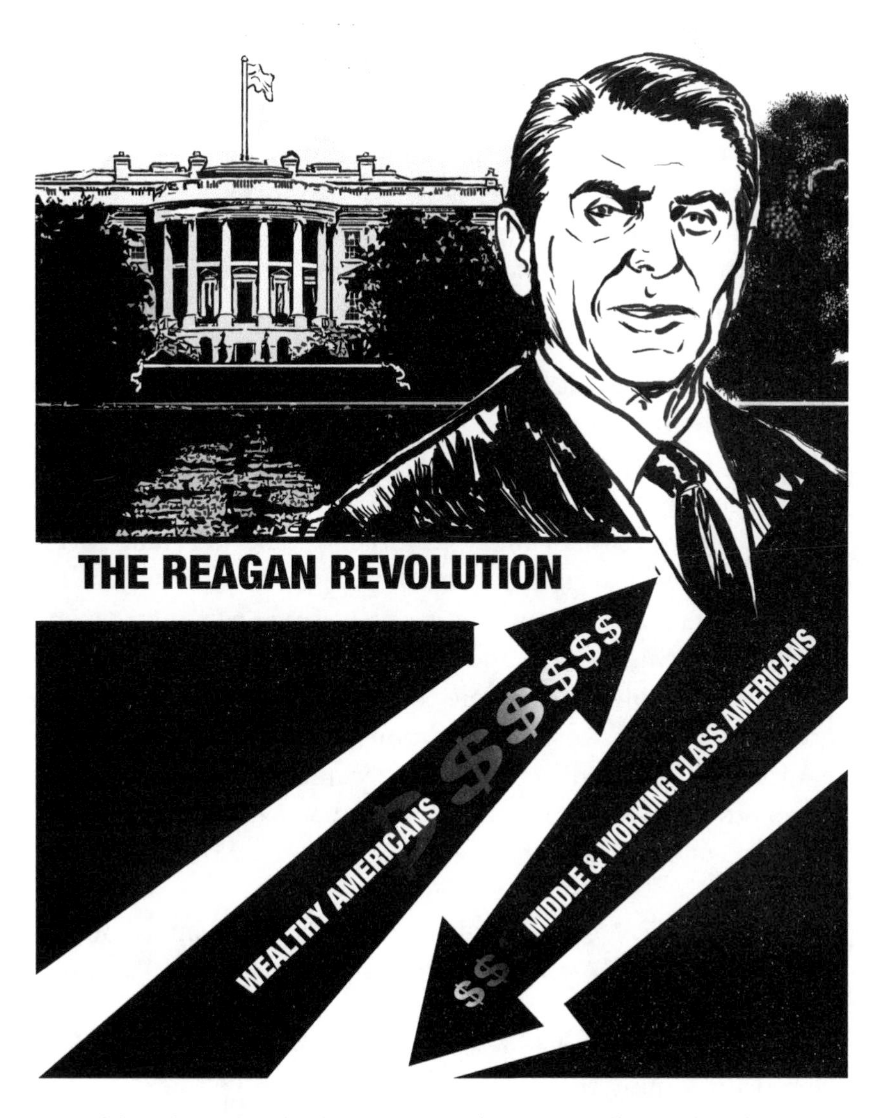

FDR liberalism reached its apex under, ironically, Richard Nixon, with the passing of environmental protection regulations, health and safety in the workplace and the Occupational Safety and Health Administration (OSHA) was established . The early 1970s consolidated some of the aspirations of the 1960s Civil Rights and anti-Vietnam War progressive movements. But it also marks the time of the sounding of the alarm among the corporate forces, who rallied and mounted a campaign to recapture lost ground in corporate power. And the campaign was remarkably successful.

Under Reagan, economic power and political power quickly moved into the right wing sphere of business. Tax cuts were given to upper income levels and the distribution of wealth began to move rapidly upward. The trend continued for 30 years until by 2011 a tiny 1 percent of the population controlled 40 percent of its wealth. The country was effectively under the control of a clique of 400 billionaires.

The Reagan Legacy

One of Ronald Reagan's first major acts as president was to fire the Federal Aviation Agency's flight controllers who had gone on strike. Reagan fired them and hired new workers to replace them. Losing the experience of all those workers had far-reaching effects on the effectiveness and safety of the flight control system for years to come. But for Reagan it was a major policy statement. He drew a line in the sand and showed that he would not tolerate strikes and would bust unions who tried to agitate for wage increases or better working conditions. It was one of the central features of Reaganism, which became the prototype of conservative government in the U.S. for the next 30-plus years. Its legacy is not hard to discern.

The effects of Reaganism could be seen early on. Noam Chomsky, in *Year 501: The Conquest Continues,* wrote in 1993, "A study released by the Economic Policy Institute on Labor Day, 1992, fleshed out the details of what people know from their experience: after a decade of Reaganism, 'most Americans are working longer hours for lower wages and considerably less security,' and 'the vast majority' are 'in many ways worse off' than in the late 1970s. From 1987, real wages have declined even for the college educated. 'Poverty rates were high by historic standards,' and 'those in poverty in 1989 were significantly poorer than the

Noam Chomsk

poor in 1979.' The poverty rate rose further in 1991, the Census Bureau reported. A congressional report released a few days later estimates that hunger has grown by 50 percent since the mid-1980s to some 30 million people. Other studies show that one of eight children under 12 suffers from hunger, a problem that reappeared in 1982 after having been overcome by government programs from the 1960s. Two researchers report that in New York, the proportion of children raised in poverty grew by 26 percent" as aid for the poor shrank during "the booming 1980s."

The Dismantling of America's Production Capability

Along with the Reagan Revolution came a revolution on Wall Street and the process of dismantling American business. The political activist Granny D Haddock described it well during a speech in Boston in 2002 that also predicted the further destruction of the American economy that was going to take place in the next years. "Mr. Reagan and those around him believed in a very new kind of American hero," said Granny D. "This new hero was a business hero — not the fellow who built up a family furniture store on Main Street and supported the Little League and the Scouts; this new hero was not the woman who worked late hours to create a successful travel agency, nor was this new business hero anything like any of the hard-working Americans who built-up our middle class, advanced our standard of living and gave us the resources and leisure for the proper civic life of a democracy... No, the Reagan business hero was the corporate takeover artist. Any regulations that might get in the way of these ruthless new capitalists were removed —removed so that reptiles of uncommon greed and brutality might rule the earth, which they now nearly do."

The demands for profit and growth on Wall Street went into a hyper mode. If a company was not meeting growth and profit expectations through its normal activities, it could be dismantled and the parts sold off to meet the requirements.

According to Granny D, "What soon happened was that ALL

corporations of medium size or larger had to look over their shoulders. How did a corporation protect itself in this environment from a hostile takeover? It had to close down any factories that were not earning obscene profits. Never mind that a factory had served a town well for a century, or that it provided a healthy and regular profit for its stockholders. If it seemed to be underperforming by the new hypergreed standards, or if it could be closed in favor of opening a foreign plant that provided a slightly higher rate of return, then, in this new atmosphere, the company was derelict in its duty to its stockholders if it did not ruthlessly act. Perfectly good and profitable factories were closed. Benefits to employees everywhere were attacked, and staffs were downsized, outsourced, computerized, downsized again, outsourced again to temp agencies that paid no health care or retirement, and on and on until America became a very different place. The gap between rich and poor is now wider than at any time in our history."

Granny D. Haddock

Once Corporate America had downsized and dismantled industries and there were no more parts to sell off, it began meeting growth expectations by cheating, faking its results, as Enron did. Then it resorted to extorting bailouts from the public at knifepoint, under the threat of an economic collapse if Congress didn't come up with the money.

The country's biggest banks also engaged in outright fraud and stealing on a wide scale. According to Thomas Friedman in the New York Times Oct. 29, 2011, "Citibank sold a package of toxic mortgage-backed securities to unsuspecting customers — securities that it knew were likely to go bust — and, with the other hand, shorted the same securities — that is, bet millions of dollars that they would go bust."

For its crimes, Citigroup was fined $285 million dollars and allowed to get away with a promise not to do it again.

Unions and Free Market Ideology

The Library of Economics and Liberty website posts "The Concise Encyclopedia of Economics" (http://www.econlib.org/library/Enc/LaborUnions.html). Its entry on Labor Unions shows the free marketer point of view on unions. It says, "Although labor unions have been celebrated in folk songs and stories as fearless champions of the downtrodden working man, this is not how economists see them. Economists who study unions—including some who are avowedly prounion—analyze them as CARTELS that raise wages above competitive levels by restricting the SUPPLY of labor to various firms and industries."

The Encyclopedia admits that, "Many unions have won higher wages and better working conditions for their members." But, however, "In doing so, however, they have reduced the number of jobs available in unionized companies. That second effect occurs because of the basic law of demand: if unions successfully raise the price of labor, employers will purchase less of it. Thus, unions are a major anticompetitive force in labor markets. Their gains come at the expense of consumers, nonunion workers, the jobless, taxpayers, and owners of corporations."

The Almighty Market

When dealing with free market ideologues it is important to remember that they speak in abstract terms that are fully real to them, more real to them than what they can reach out and touch, but which may not have much reality to other people.

Free market ideology is like a religion. It is a system of belief that is adhered to with great passion by most wealthy capitalists. It provides a rationale for greed, selfishness and corporate crime. As with other passionately held belief systems, its devotees will cling tightly to it no matter how much evidence there is against it.

The essential idea of this philosophy is that the natural principles of supply and demand in the marketplace will determine the prices of things, what people will buy and what they will pay, which businesses will survive and which will not, and there is nothing else to worry about because the market will take care of everything. Anything that any government may do to regulate the marketplace is harmful, interferes with the mysterious wisdom of the marketplace, which these ideologues look upon with more reverence than they regard anything else in heaven and earth.

There are some who believe this principle so completely that they believe that every single thing on earth, every square inch, should be privately owned, that there should be no public property of any kind, not roads, not libraries, not schools, not parks. If something cannot survive in the marketplace, that is, if it does not make money, then it should not exist. This value system is extended to the point of being applied to human beings. If you are not making enough money on which to live, no matter what the reason, you should not be able to live, according to the more extreme holders of that belief system.

Criminalizing Collective Bargaining

According to this ideology businesses should be free to do anything that will survive the marketplace. This is true no matter what it is, no matter if it destroys the community it functions in, no matter if it kills people. But in this system of belief people banding together to bargain collectively is against the rules. Under the free market ideology, collective bargaining should be outlawed, as it has been in the past, when union organizers were executed under conspiracy laws, and as it was in Wisconsin in 2011 under Governor Scott Walker and the Republican-controlled state legislature, which passed a law banning collective bargaining in state jobs.

According to this view, the capitalists can join together, combine their capital into massive corporations with great power and be granted limited liability by the government. But the workers must only deal with the owners one at a time. They cannot stand together or look out for each other's rights collectively. That's the point of view of the free marketers, the privatizers, the big capitalists, the aristocrats. And the government and the economic system are set up to support this belief system, the belief system of the aristocracy, the owners and controllers of society.

There is one underlying reality, however, that undermines all of the proselytizing about the free market of the free marketers. There is an entity in the United States called the Federal Reserve System that controls the monetary system. It is a private entity, not a government body. But it is given power by the government to control the principle monetary system of the world, the American dollar. The Federal Reserve is a whole story in itself, but the important principle in this argument is that the Federal Reserve sets the prime interest rate, which decides how much it costs to borrow money. With that power the Federal Reserve can in effect turn up or down the heat of the economy. And the way the Federal Reserve uses that power to power is slow down the economy when it gets too hot. This is necessary, say the powers that be, to prevent inflation.

Inflation means that prices rise. No one wants that, we assume, so that's fine. Actually no one minds when the prices other people pay for his goods or services go up. But we don't want to have to pay more for the things we need. So we think, what's wrong with that? Yes, it is an awesome power, in one important sense it is more than the power of the government itself. Why does this negate the arguments of the free marketers against unions?

Let's look closer at how the Federal Reserve stems inflation. According to this kind of economic reasoning, inflation is created from the bottom up. Inflation begins when the cost of labor rises. Then everything else will start to rise and the chain reaction will cause what we know as inflation. We are haunted by stories of people in Germany in the 1930s when the value of the currency plunged so fast that every day goods would cost twice what they had the day before and a whole shopping cart full of currency would be required to buy a loaf of bread.

When the free market generates so much economic activity that more jobs become available, then workers have more choices of jobs and they can ask for more pay. It becomes a seller's market for labor, the old law of supply and demand. More jobs and more choices for workers will cause employers to have to pay more for labor, so they will have to raise prices accordingly to pay the extra expense. And that will start the cycle of inflation. So when economic indicators reach a certain point, the Fed tightens the money supply, slows down the economy, slows down the flow of capital, makes investment money for business less accessible. That slows down economic activity, reduces the availability and keeps the free market from generating more jobs and forcing prices up.

This achieves the goal of keeping inflation from getting out of control. It also keeps unemployment at what the Fed and the aristocrats consider acceptable levels. In plain terms, it does not serve the purposes of the capitalist class to have full employment. It is not acceptable even if stopping it means interfering with the free market. The free marketers do not complain when the free market is interfered with to their benefit.

A society that has a mechanism built in to check the growth of the economy when it produces full employment is forcing a certain part of the population to be unemployed. If that same society refuses to provide a safety net for people who are pushed out of work by that mechanism, it then forces those people to take desperate measures to survive even though they have been pushed out of the system.

In spite of the underlying fact that the free market is artificially inhibited to the benefit of its rulers, conservatives still parrot the notion that everyone should have a job and if anyone doesn't have a job it's their own fault. And they still fall back on free market principles to justify the situation. But the argument is based on a lie. We do not have a free market and there may in fact be no such thing as a free market in the world. It's a relative notion.

Too big to Fail

The free marketers also don't mind if the free market's wisdom is thwarted in the failure of a huge bank that they deem "too big to fail." During the crash of 2008, George W. Bush's parting gift to the country as he slithered back to Texas after eight years of looting the treasury, the public was told that if a bunch of very large financial institutions went out of business it would plunge us all into a great depression from which we may never recover. It might be the end of the world as we know it. So taxpayers must bail them out.

The financial lords will not, however, bail out the taxpayers in return, even when their profits return to all-time highs a year later. Welfare is okay for large corporations that are too big to fail. For the rank and file citizen, it is free market discipline.

This game is rigged. The financial aristocracy cannot fail. If their own business decisions fail in the marketplace, the citizenry will be called to bail them out, with a knife to its throat.

In the face of a historically stacked deck in favor of those who deal the cards, who hold the power and property in society and have the power to bend the rules in their own favor, labor unions are the natural response of the workers, of the rank and file citizenry to defend themselves against the assaults on them by those who hold the power.

As corporate power has grown, people have had to band together to defend themselves against the naked grab for profit of the unrestrained corporation. As corporate power grows, labor union power should grow too, to create a balance that can protect the people from unrestrained corporate power.

The Wonderland World of Corporate Law

According to Marjorie Kelly, author of *The Divine Right of Capital,* corporate law as it now exists in America has built in inequities and fallacies that lead to severe social problems. The problems, says Kelly, are clearly spelled out on the balance sheet of a modern corporation. The corporate balance sheet shows an equation that says revenue minus costs equals profits. The costs are defined as labor plus materials. Costs are supposed to be kept low, therefore wages paid to the people who work at the corporation and are instrumental in producing its wealth, must be kept to a minimum in order to keep profits to a maximum. This is an arbitrary formulation, according to Kelly. It favors the shareholders and disregards everyone else. It could be structured differently.

Corporate law, which has evolved not through legislation but through interpretations of clever corporate lawyers that have been built into the legal system through case law in the courts, mandates that the sole function of a public corporation is to maximize the revenue to shareholders, and that is the extent of its obligation to the community. That leaves out two other parts of the community that are also deeply affected by the activities of the corporation: the people who work for the company, and the community in which the company operates.

Under the prevailing system of corporate law, the people who work for the company are considered only as an expense, similarly to the status of the workers on a feudal estate. Wages are kept as low as possible. The community in which a company is based also does not appear on a balance sheet at all. If the work of a company fouls the environment, destroys the resources of the community or makes the environment unlivable for its residents, that is of no concern to the corporation. Cleaning up after itself costs money and reduces profits, so the corporation will not do it unless it's forced to. The corporation would prefer to externalize the cost of cleaning up after itself. If GE pollutes the Hudson River, let the government clean it up, let the taxpayers shoulder the expense. It is standard practice for a corporation to externalize it every expense it can, to get if off the corporate balance sheet in order to increase profits for shareholders and fulfill its mandate.

According to Kelly, these biases favor the wealthy and are left over from an earlier age. Alexander de Tocqueville, the author of *Democracy in America*, said there are two great ages of history, the aristocratic age and the democratic age. Though it was a gradual process with many marking points, the Western world crossed the threshold into the democratic age after the American Revolution, when the English colonists used the ideas of the Enlightenment to structure a new society in which one class no longer automatically had privilege over another, and one in which governmental authority issued from the consent of the governed.

The ideals of the revolution were not necessarily followed in the real world. Most of the revolutionaries, the "Fathers of our Country", were slaveholders. That was a wild contradiction with the rhetoric of "all men are created equal." The Declaration of Independence stated an aspiration, not a realization, and many who have followed the founders have worked to push the aspirations of the founding documents farther toward realization. But others have worked to push the world back to the aristocratic period, to try to reestablish the power and legitimacy of an aristocracy. The tension between these opposite poles continues to the present day. The forces who supported slavery as an acceptable practice have their counterparts in today's world.

According to Kelly, in the post-Civil War period, the rise of the robber barons coincided with an evolution of corporate law that was rooted in the pre-democratic world. Corporations, which had been strictly limited in what they could do, were gradually altered through the courts to create the basis of a new aristocratic society. In the 19th Century corporations were opposed by conservatives because they undermined both democracy and the free market.

The tension between the aristocratic model of society and the democratic one is still with us today. In recent decades that tension is winding tighter as the extremes of wealth and poverty in the United States grow to resemble those of Third World countries.

Kelly points out that in the 20th Century, two world wars laid waste most of the monarchies of the world and by the century's end most governments were structured as democratic republics. Although political systems had crossed the line from the aristocratic age to the democratic one, economic systems are still strongly rooted in the pre-democratic world.

Kelly suggests ways to restructure corporate law to better balance the wealth among the shareholders, the producers and the surrounding community. She predicts that political democracy will be followed by political democracy in the 21st Century. De Tocqueville, who seemed nearly clairvoyant, predicted as much when he said, "Can it be believed that the democracy that has overthrown the feudal system and vanquished kings will retreat before tradesmen and capitalists?"

The Conservative Reign through Bush I, Clinton, Bush II and Obama

The Reagan Revolution continued under his successors of both parties. Reagan's vice president, George Bush, was elected for one term as president, then defeated by the Democratic challenger Bill Clinton, former governor of Arkansas.

George Bush

But though Clinton was in the

Democratic party, he was backed generously by Wall Street, the financial industry and Corporate America. Both Bush and Clinton pushed for NAFTA, the North American Free Trade Agreement. There was no candidate representing opposition to NAFTA. But the agreement just gave free rein to multinational corporations to rape the working and middle class people on both sides of the Mexican border. For Americans the Free Trade Agreements do nothing but ship jobs overseas to Third World countries where the corporations can get labor at dirt cheap prices. Cheap consumer goods are not an adequate compensation for an economy that has been broken apart and sold off for parts.

Bill Clinton

NAFTA has come to be clearly seen by working people of both the U.S. and Mexico as a knife in the back to working people. At that point the financial kingpins of the country had effectively consolidated power over both major political parties in the U.S.

By 2000 with the election between George W. Bush, the son of the previous President Bush, and Al Gore, the Supreme Court stepped in and ruled that there was no need for the people to vote at all, the Justices would save us the trouble by appointing George W. Bush president. After the court essentially struck down the right to vote for the president, the mass media, almost all of which was owned by about five corporations, stood by in silent acceptance. Americans who were outraged had nowhere to turn, no representation in the media or in the political system.

Though Bush campaigned as a "compassionate conservative" and did not even win more votes than his opponent, he took office as if he'd been swept into office on a giant wave of extreme right wing conservatism. He slashed taxes on the rich again, so they were paying less than they had even under Reagan. He launched two wars without making arrangements for financing them. Three trillion dollars were funneled through the wars in Iraq and Afghanistan to major corporations who made billions off lucrative no-bid contracts given to them by their friends in the White House. The nominal vice president, Dick Cheney, had been CEO of Halliburton during his short space of time outside of government, and when he got into the White House, his former company, of which he still owned a substantial share, suddenly received hugely lucrative contracts without having to bid against other applicants.

George W. Bush

Pouring money into the military industrial complex made that network of business very wealthy, but did not help mainstream Americans much, who continued to fall behind in income and wealth while the rich made great strides. The effect of NAFTA after nearly two decades was to gut the manufacturing sectors of the U.S. economy and send thousands of jobs to other countries where labor is cheaper. NAFTA is one element of a strategy of corporate domination of all markets in the world. It has helped to increase the profitability of corporations, but has impoverished many Americans by forcing them to compete with or lose jobs to poverty workers in Third World countries.

Removing regulations in the banking industry that were used to prevent irresponsible speculation that has historically created one financial crash after another, set the stage for the world financial meltdown of 2008. Again, laws made of, for and by corporations, have continued to increase the profits of major corporations at the cost of reducing the general welfare of the American people.

Barack Obama, a first-term U.S. senator from Illinois, captured tremendous political support when he ran for president in 2008 by effectively voicing the pent-up frustrations of the population and the urgent calls for change. Obama deftly singled out the issues that were bothering the American people, most of which centered around the fact that mainstream America had been left behind in the boom of corporate America under President George W. Bush. Obama addressed the issues that concerned the American people, promised to restore law to government, close Guantanamo prison camp, to end the war in Iraq, to stop torture as a U.S. policy. But once he got into office he appointed prominent Wall Street and financial industry kingpins to most of his cabinet posts, and one by one turned his back on most of the promises he had made during the campaign. As his campaign promises collapsed, it increasingly looked to those who had supported him and believed in his call for change, that the power that rules America had not changed hands at all. The same financial elite that created the conditions that led to a collapse were put in charge of managing during the collapse. The country went into what became glibly referred to in the mass media as a "jobless recovery," which meant that Wall Street's profits recovered quickly and were soon soaring, as the companies that

Barack Obama

were bailed out by taxpayers lavished giant bonuses on banking system insiders, and an increasing number of mainstream Americans lost their homes, their jobs, their pensions.

Republican legislators, who represent Corporate America even more than Democratic legislators, decided that after taxpayers had bailed out the giant financial institutions that were supposedly too big to fail without destroying the entire system, it was time to balance the budget, not by making the perpetrators of the widespread banking fraud pay, but by taking money out of the country's hard earned Social Security and Medicare safety nets. Obama, though a Democrat supposedly representing a more liberal view of government, stood by and cooperated with Republicans who wanted to cut Social Security and Medicare, in effect giving Wall Street what it had not been able to accomplish even under the extreme right wing administration of George W. Bush. Obama became the perfect right wing enabler, the perfect foil.

With the media and political elite effectively corralled into the corporate camp, the vast majority of the country no longer had any legitimate channels for exercising their political rights as defined by our Constitution and legal system. After an increasing number of people found themselves marginalized and without choices, the pent up frustration finally erupted on September 17, 2011.

Deregulation of the Financial Markets and the Great Recession

The regulations on financial markets put into effect under Roosevelt were effective in stabilizing financial markets to a high degree. What had been a cycle of devastating depressions in a boom-and-bust cycle that swung around every decade or so, became a more moderate business cycle. After the Great Depression there were no more depressions, no more cataclysmic financial calamities as had been common under unregulated capitalism. The business cycle was tamer. Recessions came and went periodically, but the devastating financial collapses that happened every decade or so under unregulated capitalism became things of the past. But under the conservative resurgence that started in the 1970s and continued under both Democratic and Republican presidents, the regulations of the New Deal were gradually unraveled. Financial markets became freer, and wilder than ever before, leading to a financial calamity in 2008 that was nearly on par with the Great Depression.

After three years under the Obama administration, little had been done to rein in the excesses of Wall Street and Corporate America. In the face of scandalous reports of massive corporate swindles and thievery, none of the criminals went to jail. Almost no action was taken against the outrages of Wall Street. In October 2011 Citibank had to pay a $285 million fine to settle a case in which it had sold toxic mortgage-backed securities to customers under the pretense of their being good investments, and then secretly shorted the securities, which means they bet that the securities would fail in the casino of Wall Street. The crime involved $1 billion worth of assets that the bank knowingly dumped on its customers knowing they would fail. This is only one of a long list of corporate crimes committed by the very institutions that were bailed out by taxpayers. And yet none of the criminals had to be accountable for their actions. No bankers went to jail, but of those whose outrage drove them into the street to protest Wall Street's sleazy deals, thousands were jailed and or beaten.

Chapter Seven:

Occupy Wall Street and the 21st Century Resurgence of the People's Movements

With the Occupy Wall Street movement that kicked off with a full time presence in Zuccotti Park near Wall Street in Lower Manhattan on September 17, 2011, the dynamics of labor organizing came together with Civil Rights and antiwar activism to create a broad based resistance movement, conceived up as representative of the 99 percent of the people who have been left behind by the corporate-controlled economic system since the onset of the Reagan Revolution. By October 31 1,039 Occupy

Wall Street demonstrations had taken place in 87 countries. It was a movement that spread like wild fire.

In the year before he died, historian Howard Zinn was interviewed by The Real News network and he said that a reinvigorated union movement would be needed to bring about the kind of social change that was needed in the US. He did point out, however, that the Civil Rights movement and the anti-Vietnam War movements in the 1960s accomplished significant objectives without support from labor unions. "There is energy beyond the workplace for the creation of a social movement," said Zinn. "There is energy in the communities, in the neighborhoods, among consumers. Consumers have the power of the boycott, which is tantamount to the power of the strike, in that they can bring a large corporation to its knees, to make the nation stand up and take notice."

In the early 21st Century, only a small part of the work force, and an even smaller proportion of the population, is organized into unions. "That's the situation we were in the 1930s," said Zinn. "Labor was just the AFL, and they organized a very small part of the workforce. It wasn't until the CIO, first the Committee for Industrial Organization within the AFL, and later the Congress of Industrial Organization outside the AFL, organized all the groups that were shunned by the AFL, because they were unskilled workers, they were immigrants, they were blacks, they were women, and they were unorganized. Today 90 percent of the workforce is unorganized. They are organizable. This 90 percent of the workforce are not people who are rich. They are people who need unions. They need to raise their wages. They need to face their employers with some strength, rather than the weakness of an individual facing a corporation. So there is a reservoir of possibility there for organizing. What will it take? I don't know. It will take an enormous initiative."

As 2011 drew to a close, it turned out to be a watershed year for the union movement. As the corporatocracy, led by billionaires like the Koch brothers, prepared to move in for the final strike to eliminate unions from American life by attacking the right to engage in collective bargaining itself for state government employees. Wisconsin Governor Scott Walker used his Republican majority in the state legislature to pass laws making it illegal for state employees to engage in collective bargaining at all. The people of Wisconsin, including its unions, mounted a ferocious counterattack, launching recall elections for several of the legislators who voted to outlaw unions. Six Republican legislators were put up for recall. The end result was that two Republicans were forced to give up their seats to Democratic challengers. The recall brought Democrats within one vote of controlling the legislature. The Republicans retained a margin of one vote, but one Republican legislature was a moderate who did not rubber stamp the right wing agenda of the governor. So it nullified Governor Walker's capacity to ram through any bills he wanted to.

Ohio's newly elected Republican Governor John Kasich also pushed through a bill outlawing unions for government employees. The Ohio law went even further than the Wisconsin law by including police and firefighters in its ban on collective bargaining. But pro-labor forces in a coalition called We Are Ohio led a campaign to put the issue on the ballot in a referendum and the law was struck down by a huge majority, 61 percent for repealing the bill versus 39 for leaving it in place. The election result reflected the results of a New York Times/CBS News poll that showed that Americans opposed weakening the bargaining rights of public employee unions by a margin of nearly two to one: 60 percent to 33 percent. The humbled Governor Kasich said, "It's clear the people have spoken. My viewpoint is when the people speak in a campaign like this and a referendum, you have to listen when you're a public servant. This requires me to take a deep breath and spend some time reflecting on what happened here."

AFL-CIO President Richard Trumka said, "Today's defeat of Issue 2 is a major victory for working families in Ohio and across the country. Ohio's working people successfully fought back against lies pushed by shadowy multi-national corporations and their anonymous front groups that attempted to scapegoat public service employees and everyone they serve by assaulting collective bargaining rights."

With a majority of Americans in polls saying they supported the cause of the Occupy Wall Street movement, and unions signing on with their support, many wondered if the long-awaited galvanization and resurgence of the union movement had finally begun.

Wisconsin AFL Secretary-Treasurer Stephanie Bloomingdale, said, "This vote is a lightning bolt of hope across Ohio and Wisconsin and everywhere right-wing governors are trying to take away the rights of workers... The mood is very good, people are really enthused, seeing this as a pivot point. It's a hairpin turn for labor, symbolizing a revival of American labor."

Indeed, with the uniting of such a broad swath of the American public in a single focused campaign against the excessive power of Wall Street over our society, it seemed that the possibility of a new level of union organizing that would unite previously separated sectors, such as labor, civil rights activists, antiwar activists, and unorganized independent citizens. In 2011, at this juncture of history, the power of union organizing is once again demanded urgently, but the kind of organizing for social change that will be necessary for this wave of history will necessarily be different from the unions of the past.

In the 99 Percent movement, the constituencies that were not united during the Vietnam or Civil Rights periods, find themselves united against a single opposition. Corporate financial power has become so concentrated, with an inordinate amount of political power in the hands of a few hundred billionaire power players, that it presents a single target.

The drive for corporate power and wealth would not, could not moderate itself, and it finally destroyed itself by overreaching.

Wall Street's insensitivity to the people its policies were destroying led it to commit ever more flagrant crimes, while the political power structure did nothing to rein them in, and finally the top just blew off the pressure cooker.

It is hard to pinpoint the exact moment in which the new movement coalesced, but some young radical Americans said, "Let's Occupy Wall Street." After initial attempts to bully the protestors into leaving with huge military style police attacks on them only served to rouse more support for the movement from across America, the authorities backed down and tried to regroup and consider new strategies. The leaderless movement could not be decapitated. But the question remained, where would the movement go?

Unions, politicians, political parties, lobbyists and corporate leaders all sought to discover how to respond to the movement, and how to gain advantage from it. And those who support the movement's basic principles of fairness in economics and government must figure out what they can do to best contribute to the movement, or how best to further their own interests in concert with millions of others with closely aligned interests.

At the time of this writing, these are the momentous changes that are being considered and reckoned with by all these sectors. New kinds of organizing will be required, and will be created. It remains to be seen what forms they will take. But union history has always followed a varied, meandering course, as it has followed the course of history. The history of unions reflects the diversity of the working people who needed them and created them through history. They took many different forms as they evolved with each boom-and-bust cycle, each financial catastrophe and the economic pressure on regular people they created.

In the past unions may have represented laborers: miners, railroad workers, agricultural workers. The term "labor union" connotes physical labor. But in fact, whether workers swing a shovel, push a pencil or sit in front of computers, the same kinds of issues arise in a capitalist society dominated by big corporations. As Americans have fallen out of unions over recent decades, they have become more vulnerable, and the old issues of worker versus capital raise their ugly heads again.

Americans were complacent for a long time when the country had produced the most prosperous middle class in history. In the aftermath of the crash of 2008, with more and more people being pushed out of homes and jobs, America may finally have reached the long-awaited tipping point that Howard Zinn referred to when he talked about "an enormous initiative."

The emergence of the Occupy Wall Street movement suddenly provided a common focal point for many separate sectors of society. The time was ripe, apparently, and the OWS action seemed to serve as the required catalyst, the single piece of dust on a windowpane that sets off a crystallization that instantly covers the entire pane.

We have yet to see what kinds of new organizations, new alignments and new power blocs will emerge as the people's struggle against the corporate oligarchy takes shape and begins to mature. The common focal point is in itself enormously powerful because, as Zinn said above, millions of people have power as consumers to bring corporations to their knees very quickly if their reluctance to buy stops the profits from pouring into the corporations coffers. New methods of applying power will be devised.

The Move Your Money action, set originally for November 8, 2011, succeeded in getting 650,000 people to close their accounts at some of the predatory giant financial institutions. But the organizers of the action found out quickly that moving one's money was not something people could rush into. The movement did not have the effect initially that might have been expected if as many people moved their money as expressed their inclination to do so in polls and surveys.

Even if only 54 percent polled support the so-called 99 Percent, 54 percent of 280 million people is 150 million. If they went a day without buying a certain product, for example, it would send a massive shockwave through the corporate world. Americans, when their backs were pushed to the wall, realized that they do in fact have power. That is the beginning of the new wave of unions in America. The unions of tomorrow may not be the unions of today. They may not even be organized along the same conceptual lines. But it seems clear now in late 2011 that the resurgence of the union movement has begun.

Appendix

Rules for Radicals

How activist organizations achieve their goals

Over the generations, union activists developed a variety of techniques for organizing and exercising power for working people to win their objectives in their conflicts with powerful employers. Alinsky introduced the principles by saying, "In this book we are concerned with how to create mass organizations to seize power and give it to the people; to realize the democratic dream of equality, justice, peace.... 'Better to die on your feet than to live on your knees.'"

The power alluded to in these principles for radicals is democratic power, the power of greater numbers, and the power of law. But although the democratic principle and law are unquestionably part of the foundation of the United States of America, which was in fact founded on a rebellion, they must be activated in order to take effect in society. The actual power underlying status quo society is economic power, and that status quo always stands in the way of bringing reform that will better incorporate the principles of democracy and justice that are formulated by the American Constitution. Activist principles seek to find ways to actualize democratic power as a force to resist the superior economic power of the business ownership class. Rules for Radicals compiles the lore of generations of activists who found ways to agitate for their rights and to bring democratic principles into the actual workings of society.

Many of these techniques were compiled by organizer Saul Alinsky. His book *Rules for Radicals* has been read by many community organizers, including Barack Obama, as a good primer in activism.

Alinsky's rules include the following:

- Power is not only what you have but what your adversary thinks you have.
- Never go outside the experience of your people.
- Whenever possible, go outside of the experience of the adversary.
- Make the adversary live up to their own book of rules.
- Ridicule is man's most potent weapon.
- A good tactic is one that your people enjoy.
- A tactic that drags on too long becomes a drag.
- Keep the pressure on with different tactics and actions.
- Utilize all events of the period for your purpose.
- The threat is usually more terrifying than the thing itself.
- Develop operations that maintain constant pressure on the opposition.
- If you push a negative hard enough, it breaks through to its counterside.
- The price of a successful attack is a constructive alternative.
- Pick the target, freeze it, personalize it, and polarize it.

THE FOR BEGINNERS® SERIES

AFRICAN HISTORY FOR BEGINNERS:	ISBN 978-1-934389-18-8
ANARCHISM FOR BEGINNERS:	ISBN 978-1-934389-32-4
ARABS & ISRAEL FOR BEGINNERS:	ISBN 978-1-934389-16-4
ART THEORY FOR BEGINNERS:	ISBN 978-934389-47-8
ASTRONOMY FOR BEGINNERS:	ISBN 978-934389-25-6
AYN RAND FOR BEGINNERS:	ISBN 978-1-934389-37-9
BARACK OBAMA FOR BEGINNERS, AN ESSENTIAL GUIDE:	ISBN 978-1-934389-44-7
BLACK HISTORY FOR BEGINNERS:	ISBN 978-1-934389-19-5
THE BLACK HOLOCAUST FOR BEGINNERS:	ISBN 978-1-934389-03-4
BLACK WOMEN FOR BEGINNERS:	ISBN 978-1-934389-20-1
CHOMSKY FOR BEGINNERS:	ISBN 978-1-934389-17-1
DADA & SURREALISM FOR BEGINNERS:	ISBN 978-1-934389-00-3
DANTE FOR BEGINNERS:	ISBN 978-1-934389-67-6
DECONSTRUCTION FOR BEGINNERS:	ISBN 978-1-934389-26-3
DEMOCRACY FOR BEGINNERS:	ISBN 978-1-934389-36-2
DERRIDA FOR BEGINNERS:	ISBN 978-1-934389-11-9
EASTERN PHILOSOPHY FOR BEGINNERS:	ISBN 978-1-934389-07-2
EXISTENTIALISM FOR BEGINNERS:	ISBN 978-1-934389-21-8
FDR AND THE NEW DEAL FOR BEGINNERS:	ISBN 978-1-934389-50-8
FOUCAULT FOR BEGINNERS:	ISBN 978-1-934389-12-6
GLOBAL WARMING FOR BEGINNERS:	ISBN 978-1-934389-27-0
HEIDEGGER FOR BEGINNERS:	ISBN 978-1-934389-13-3
ISLAM FOR BEGINNERS:	ISBN 978-1-934389-01-0
JANE AUSTEN FOR BEGINNERS:	ISBN 978-1-934389-61-4
JUNG FOR BEGINNERS:	ISBN 978-1-934389-76-8
KIERKEGAARD FOR BEGINNERS:	ISBN 978-1-934389-14-0
LACAN FOR BEGINNERS:	ISBN 978-1-934389-39-3
LINGUISTICS FOR BEGINNERS:	ISBN 978-1-934389-28-7
MALCOLM X FOR BEGINNERS:	ISBN 978-1-934389-04-1
MARX'S *DAS KAPITAL* FOR BEGINNERS:	ISBN 978-1-934389-59-1
MCLUHAN FOR BEGINNERS:	ISBN 978-1-934389-75-1
NIETZSCHE FOR BEGINNERS:	ISBN 978-1-934389-05-8
THE OLYMPICS FOR BEGINNERS:	ISBN 978-1-934389-33-1
PHILOSOPHY FOR BEGINNERS:	ISBN 978-1-934389-02-7
PLATO FOR BEGINNERS:	ISBN 978-1-934389-08-9
POETRY FOR BEGINNERS:	ISBN 978-1-934389-46-1
POSTMODERNISM FOR BEGINNERS:	ISBN 978-1-934389-09-6
RELATIVITY & QUANTUM PHYSICS FOR BEGINNERS	ISBN 978-1-934389-42-3
SARTRE FOR BEGINNERS:	ISBN 978-1-934389-15-7
SHAKESPEARE FOR BEGINNERS:	ISBN 978-1-934389-29-4
STRUCTURALISM & POSTSTRUCTURALISM FOR BEGINNERS:	ISBN 978-1-934389-10-2
WOMEN'S HISTORY FOR BEGINNERS:	ISBN 978-1-934389-60-7
U.S. CONSTITUTION FOR BEGINNERS:	ISBN 978-1-934389-62-1
ZEN FOR BEGINNERS:	ISBN 978-1-934389-06-5
ZINN FOR BEGINNERS:	ISBN 978-1-934389-40-9

www.forbeginnersbooks.com

The Boundlessness of
the Universe
The Limitlessness of
the Spirit
The Stark Poetry at
the Most Challenging Frontier
of Human Knowledge . . .

"Space opera as Stapledon would have written it, had he the knack."

—*Chicago Tribune*

"Each new novel only serves to illustrate how masterful Bear has become. ETERNITY hurtles the reader into a delightful, if occasionally dizzying, series of adventures that explore the very nature of time and space along the way. Alien invaders, alternate universes and mathematical marvels jostle each other for the reader's attention while Bear rockets the story ever onward and upward with a fast-paced narrative and deftly drawn characters."

—*Houston Post*

"Striking."

—*Publishers Weekly*

"Bear is one of the few SF writers capable of following where Olaf Stapledon led, beyond the limits of mere human ambition and geological time."

—*Locus*

"Imaginative."

—*Kirkus Reviews*

Also by Greg Bear
Available from Warner Books

Anvil of Stars
Queen of Angels
Strength of Stones
Tangents
The Wind from a Burning Woman

GREG BEAR

ETERNITY

A Time Warner Company

WARNER BOOKS EDITION

Cover design by Don Puckey
Cover illustration by Bob Eggleton
Hand lettering by Carl Dellacroce

Warner Books, Inc.
1271 Avenue of the Americas
New York, NY 10020

A Time Warner Company

Printed in the United States of America

Originally published in hardcover by Warner Books.
First Printed in Paperback: November, 1989
Reissued: December, 1994